Management
in Two Cultures

Revised Edition

Management
in Two Cultures

Revised Edition

Bridging the Gap
between U.S. and
Mexican Managers

Eva S. Kras

INTERCULTURAL PRESS, INC.

For information, contact:
Intercultural Press, Inc.
P.O. Box 700
Yarmouth, Maine 04096 USA

© 1995 by Intercultural Press

Book design by Patty J. Topel
Cover illustration by Lois Leonard Stock

Printed in the United States of America

99 98 97   2 3 4 5

Library of Congress Cataloging-in-Publication Data

Kras, Eva S. (Eva Simonsen)
    Management in two cultures : bridging the gap between U.S. and Mexican Managers / Eva S. Kras.—Rev. ed.
        p.   cm.
    Includes bibliographical references.
    ISBN 1-877864-32-3
    1. Communication in personnel management—Mexico. 2. Communication in personnel management—United States. 3. Communication in personnel management—Cross-cultural studies. 4. Offshore assembly industry—Mexico.   I. Title

HF5549.5.C6K73 1995
658.4'5—dc   94-34342
                                                     CIP

Table of Contents

Acknowledgments

This book started with an idea which I felt would help business managers from two countries I admire very much—the United States and Mexico. As the idea grew, I was encouraged by Professor Roger Chartier of the Universidad Autónoma de Guadalajara, who expressed his confidence in my ability to write it. But first I had to do the research and gather the data I needed, which meant going through the complex process of identifying key executives and setting up the interviews which were to provide the information on which the book would be based. To reach the people I wanted and gain their confidence, I needed introductions. I am deeply indebted to Roberto Santa Cruz, Adolf Horn, and José Luís Reyes for providing those introductions, without which this book would have been impossible.

I must also, of course, express my sincere appreciation to all of the executives I interviewed. They contributed freely of their time and knowledge, and their enthusiasm for the book helped me to continue when difficulties seemed insurmountable.

In addition I would like to acknowledge the invaluable contribution made by those who critiqued the first draft of the manuscript. They included, again, Roberto Santa Cruz, Adolf Horn, and José Luís Reyes, along with Enrique Luis González Garza, Clifford Cameron, Enrique Lazcano, Hugh Smiley, and Alan Rogers. A special note of thanks must also go to Virginia Sully for correcting my many errors.

Finally, I want to express my indebtedness to my ever understanding and supportive husband, who served as critic and helper. And my profound thanks go to David Hoopes, my editor, who showed unfailing understanding and patience as he skillfully guided me over the many hurdles of this project.

This book is the product of the experience, knowledge, and opinions of many people on both sides of the border, and I have tried my best to do justice to their contributions.

Foreword to
the Revised Edition

This new edition of *Management in Two Cultures* finds Mexico going through a period of rapid change. Mexico's entry into GATT (General Agreement on Tariffs and Trade) in the late 1980s began to drive the country into the world marketplace. That process is being accelerated with the creation of NAFTA (North American Free Trade Agreement). As a result, many businesses have had to go through painful restructuring and modernization of their operations in order to survive. Hundreds of companies, mainly small ones, have gone bankrupt and indications are that many more will follow.

What effect have these rapid changes had on the cultural base of businesses in Mexico?

An interesting phenomenon is taking place among Mexican leaders in companies which have modernized. These executives are engaged in an intense soul-searching regarding the roots of their organizational and operational philosophies and the deep cultural values of their country. In doing so, they have sought to separate those values from more superficial customs and behaviors which they realize interfere with efficient operations and must be modified or discarded. The deeper values are invariably person-oriented and involve a participative form of management. The actual style which is emerging is a mixture of a number of foreign influences which have been adapted to Mexican values and perspectives.

How do these changes affect U.S. and other foreign companies working in Mexico? First, they should be aware of the direction in which the thinking of Mexican management is developing and appreciate the strong influence which culture will continue to have on business in Mexico. Values related to family and interpersonal relations are the ones which will be the most important to respect for foreign companies coming to Mexico.

With Mexico's entry into NAFTA there will be great pressure on Mexican management to conform to and adopt management practices from other countries. Undoubtedly, many Mexican managers will try, and some will certainly succeed. But these changes will for the most part be relatively superficial, such as respect for time constraints and more effort at quality control. Therefore, foreign companies interested in providing a working environment which reaps maximum benefit for their employees and maximum profits for themselves in the long term must consider carefully how to deal effectively with Mexicans, both in the framework of their day-to-day behaviors in the workplace and in the context of the deep immutable values of the culture. It has been the intention of this book to provide the foreign, especially the U.S., business executive guidance in achieving those goals. We believe the revisions and updating done for this edition sharpen the focus and make it even more valuable for Mexicans and Americans as they engage in a mutually fruitful adaptation process.

Mr. Wygard's Story

This true story was told to me, not long before his death, by the late Edward J. Wygard, O.B.E., then director of Arthur D. Little Mexicana, S.A. de C.V. It serves to illustrate some of the problems a foreign business executive faces when operating in Mexico.

Mr. Wygard came to Mexico from England about 1950 and established a milk pasteurization plant. For eight months he tried every way possible to convince his workers of the importance of punctuality and of checking every detail of their work. He stressed repeatedly that the milk would spoil if left too long or if the vats were not properly cleaned. The response was always, "Yes, yes, we will do our best," but nothing changed.

Then one day an impressive new pasteurization unit arrived and was duly installed. To celebrate the occasion, Mr. Wygard decided to throw a big party at the plant. The employees did most of the planning and draped the new unit with garlands. It was a very special occasion.

The party was a great success and everybody had a good time. During the party one of Mr. Wygard's key supervisors took him aside and said, "Now we see that you are buena gente.* *From now on I am sure everyone will really try to do their best for you." And so it was. Neither punctuality nor quality checks were any longer a problem. He had won their confidence.*

This happened a long time ago, but given the persistence of cultural traditions in Mexico, it could have happened yesterday.

---

*Literally, a "good person," one you can trust and have as a friend.

Mr. Wygard was not American, but he was a highly gifted businessman nurtured in the Anglo-Saxon tradition, and his approach was very much like that of managers from the United States. That Mr. Wygard was later chosen to head the operations in Mexico of the highly respected international consulting firm, Arthur D. Little, bears witness to his acumen and adaptability to an entirely different business environment.

Introduction

Though Mexicans and Americans have been involved in business dealings with each other for many decades, each has persistently experienced difficulty in understanding and accepting how the other thinks and feels. This book attempts to dispel some of the mystery surrounding their different approaches to essentially similar goals. We make no pretense that it constitutes an in-depth psychological study. Instead, it is an effort to get at the practical implications that deeply rooted cultural differences have for international business relationships. Based on concepts widely accepted by anthropologists and cross-cultural communication specialists, it examines, through a comparative study of the culturally conditioned differences in management styles, key areas in which conflict and misunderstanding occur in business communication and personal interaction between Mexicans and Americans. The cultural differences—in values, behavior patterns, ways of thinking, etc.—that lie behind these conflicts and misunderstandings are discussed, and guidelines for surmounting them proposed. Much of the data is drawn from a series of in-depth interviews with both Mexican and U.S. senior executives (see appendix B for a description of the research methodology).

Mexico is a country undergoing rapid and profound change, not only from the standpoint of business practices, but also in its everyday customs, mores, and values. The greatest influence on these changes is beyond doubt exerted by the United States, where a highly developed consumer economy is seen as the key to progress and affluence, and hence to happiness. As a result, traditional Mexican values are being eroded, and there is a gradual shift toward an increasingly materialistic ethos. However, in spite of the changing fabric of Mexican society, there is a strong feeling among the members of the business community that cultural differences between the two peoples are a major hurdle to effective communication and will remain so for generations to come.

It has long been recognized that culture plays a distinct role in management and that management styles vary markedly from culture to culture. It has not been as easy, however, to identify the specific differences which cause misunderstandings across cultures or to put forth recommendations as to how these misunderstandings can be avoided. It is our intent here to address these issues and, especially, to put into the hands of Mexican and U.S. business executives a practical tool for bridging the cultural gap that exists between them.

This book will be of particular use to those from the United States who are:

1. executives of multinational companies in Mexico or who are about to begin such an assignment,

2. executives with U.S. (or Canadian) firms which have branches in Mexico or which have relations with Mexican firms,

3. executives with firms in other Latin American countries (though local cultural variations will have to be taken into account), and

4. educators and students specializing in Latin American business studies.

In the case of Canadians, especially Francophones, differences between their own culture and that of the United States will also have to be taken into account. Nevertheless, Canadians in general and Anglophones in particular will undoubtedly encounter many of the problems discussed in this book and will find here useful insights and recommendations.

Because of the methodology used (interviews with experienced business executives) and the style of presentation (an exchange of correspondence and extensive use of real events and incidents), culturally unprepared readers from the United

States or Canada should see themselves reflected rather vividly in the eyes of their Mexican counterparts. On the other side, Mexican executives can gain insights into the mentality of their northern neighbors while also seeing themselves reflected in the eyes of U.S. business executives.

There is always a risk in cross-cultural analysis of stereotyping your subjects. One cannot compare culturally-based behaviors and attitudes without making generalizations. The reader must understand that when we say that the societies of Mexico and the United States have certain cultural characteristics, we mean characteristics which are strong, pervasive, or even dominant but not necessarily universal. We realize that each person is unique, that each culture encompasses all possible cultural characteristics, and that nowhere will one find the perfectly "typical" American or Mexican. This lesson is, of course, especially important in the actual face-to-face encounter where one meets not a stereotype but a person who, while sharing certain traits with his or her cultural compatriots, is nevertheless a unique human being.

Another pitfall of comparative culture study lies in attempting to determine whether given characteristics are right or wrong, good or bad. Such efforts are of very little use in the process of cross-cultural analysis since the person making the judgment is inescapably steeped in his or her own culture and finds it almost impossible to separate out subjective and objective aspects of the judgment.

In our interviews, for instance, various U.S. executives quoted well-worn cliches such as:

1. "What works in the United States ought to work in Mexico." But one cannot transplant U.S. methods and management techniques indiscriminately and expect them to work as they do in the United States.

2. "What is new and modern is the most effective." But just because a concept is new and modern does not guarantee its effectiveness in a different environment.

3. "U.S. management methods are right, and Mexican wrong." But there are many excellent Mexican organizations which have outstanding performance records and human relations policies, while still remaining distinctly Mexican.

In the end most of the executives interviewed agreed that what was important was to recognize that while the two management styles are different and may be more or less effective in achieving certain aims under certain conditions, one cannot be said to be "right" or the other "wrong" in any general sense.

The Different Faces of Mexico

Before going on to the substance of the book, it may be helpful to Canadian and U.S. readers to sketch briefly what might be called the "different faces of Mexico." From a distance it is easy to think of a foreign country, even one so near, as essentially uniform, as a single entity describable in a certain limited set of terms, such as one might encounter in a simple geographic summary. Such descriptions never capture the reality of a country and its people.

Mexico is a country of extremes. It has extremes in climate from the temperate north to the hot, humid, tropical southeast, and it has extremes in terrain from great mountain ranges and high plateaus to flat dry plains and steamy jungles. These extremes are matched by extremes in the types of people who inhabit the country—from the industrious north to the traditional southeast. In terms of the business and industrial communities, Mexico can usefully be divided into four distinct regions:

1. The north with its center in Monterrey
2. The central region with its center in Guadalajara
3. The southeast, which includes such areas as Oaxaca and Yucatán
4. The metropolitan region of the capital, Mexico City

There is a fifth region of great importance which deserves a study of its own: the oil-rich states along the Gulf of Mexico. While these states share some of the problems of the rest of the republic, their dependence on one commodity and its derivatives for over two generations has to some extent set them apart.

I have therefore deliberately excluded them from this study.

Monterrey, the center of the northern region, is a sophisticated city of about five million inhabitants with many years of experience with heavy industry. Its people are hardworking and aggressive. These characteristics are generally attributed to three main influences. First, their ancestors came from a region of Spain noted for the industriousness of its population. They were extremely isolated from the capital of New Spain (Mexico City) and thus developed an independent spirit which they maintain to this day. Second, the inhospitable terrain and harsh climate, with its cold winters and hot, dry summers, has had a significant influence. Eking out a living has always been a struggle, and survival meant planning ahead. Third, many observers believe its proximity to the United States has resulted in the absorption, to a degree, of the U.S. work ethic. The cities along the U.S. border, while forming part of this region, nevertheless constitute a special case, since they have in recent years become the home of vigorous and growing foreign-owned industries under the *maquiladora* program. The maquiladoras are off-shore, foreign-owned (mainly U.S.) companies, and the regulations related to their status are now changing due to NAFTA. This sets them apart from other areas of Mexico, and they will be dealt with in more detail later.

In the central region, which extends as far as León and Irapuato in the neighboring state of Guanajuato, Guadalajara is the largest and most important center. It was, until a few years ago, a quiet, relaxed town with only small and medium-sized, family-owned businesses. However, the complexion of the city has changed in recent years. Guadalajara has seen a marked increase in the number of medium-sized industries as well as the establishment of a few large corporations and multinationals, increasing the influx of population from other states, including a considerable number from Mexico City following the 1985 earthquake. It is now a bustling city with a vital business and industrial core and a metropolitan population of approximately five million. Nonetheless, most executives in Guadalajara are still relatively easygoing. The atmosphere continues to reflect the tradition of the family business, grown larger perhaps, yet still run mostly in a conservative, autocratic style. However, in the few large organizations which operate in this region, more sophisticated management methods are in evidence.

In the southeast, which includes among others the states of Oaxaca and Yucatán, there is little industry, and the business approach is almost wholly traditional, paternalistic, and autocratic. The people themselves are relaxed and slow-moving. It is a mountainous region with a tropical climate and large indigenous populations which have preserved almost intact their centuries-old traditions.

Last, there is the booming metropolis and capital, Mexico City and its environs. Here the cosmopolitan atmosphere naturally has a significant effect on the way business and industry are managed. It also makes for a more fast-moving and dynamic environment. At the same time there has been a massive influx of poor, illiterate countryfolk in search of work. The result is a city (now the largest in the world) teeming with many more people than its infrastructure can handle, a vast part of whom live in the worst of slum conditions. Meanwhile, the city center and the major industrial areas appear full of vitality, and a dynamic cadre of business executives has emerged. This group has close contacts with the international business community, which has greatly influenced its business outlook and approach. Nevertheless, the environmental and social problems resulting from the sheer size of Mexico City create an atmosphere of stress and tension for all who live there. This situation has been further aggravated by the tragic earthquake which devastated the center of Mexico City in September 1985.

The Border Area and the *Maquiladoras*

The border area is a special region. On the one hand, it is dynamic and changing. On the other hand, it is an area where cross-cultural contact between Mexicans and Americans is widespread and intense, so that the acquisition by both of the knowledge and skills discussed in the pages that follow may be even more critical than elsewhere in the country.

Just across the border from the United States, Mexico has been encouraging the development of maquiladoras, labor-intensive foreign-owned industries which assemble products for export to other countries. Presently there are over two thousand maquiladoras, and the structure of the maquiladora concept is changing due to the gradual removal of tariff barriers with the entry of Mexico, Canada, and the United States into NAFTA. But the advantages for foreign companies of being able easily to operate 100-percent foreign-owned companies within Mexican borders remain attractive. Therefore, these types of companies will likely continue to exist for the foreseeable future.

The Mexican border cities, especially the two largest, Ciudad Juárez and Tijuana, have grown from small, quiet towns into bustling urban centers within a span of a very few years. This expansion, stimulated by the maquiladoras, has led to a massive influx of workers, profoundly altering the composition of their populations and placing their infrastructures and services under tremendous strain. It has also meant that their economies are dominated by the maquiladora industry, thus placing their people in a position of direct economic dependence on the United States, since the majority of maquiladoras are U.S.-owned and -managed.

This influx of U.S. investment and management has exerted a considerable influence on the Mexican executives working along the border. They have learned to accept and even adopt a great deal of the U.S. management outlook and approach. Mostly, they feel a certain pride in having learned to do things "the American way," and in many respects they consider themselves more advanced than their counterparts in the interior of Mexico insofar as attitudes toward the more critical aspects of modern management techniques are concerned.

At the same time there is a deep, although sometimes concealed, sense of national and cultural identity in this management group, based on a firm attachment to their cultural values. One executive expressed it this way: "We are very different from the Americans, and we do not want to lose our values and culture. But because the Americans cannot understand how we think and feel, we have to learn to do things their way."

One thus finds among the Mexican managers a mixture of pride in their ability to accept and learn foreign ways and their desire to remain Mexican. Many feel that the Mexicans along the border are probably more nationalistic than people elsewhere in the republic because it is the only way they can avoid being swallowed up by Uncle Sam.

Part I

Two Letters

The letters which follow are fictional but represent a broad spectrum of management attitudes, both of U.S. managers and their Mexican counterparts (in most cases subordinate managers), who are part of the Mexican business scene. On the whole they are designed to provoke thinking on both sides.

The difference in outlook of these two executives will be obvious, revealed not only in the values they express, but in their different approaches to management. A number of obstacles stand in the way of their establishing effective working relationships. One lies in differences in customary behaviors and the effect these have on everyday communication. Another lies in the very different way they think about problems and approach everyday issues. Note in particular how confrontational situations are accepted or rejected and how misunderstandings are allowed to go unaddressed, with a resulting adverse impact on the relationship.

It is important to remember that in these letters, as elsewhere, stereotypes or composite characters appear which will probably not be encountered in real life. Indeed, those U.S. executives who are by nature and training considerate, sensitive, and friendly experience fewer problems in Mexico, though they do appear to be the exception. Also, the severity of the problems encountered depends to a great extent on the amount of exposure the Mexican executive has had to U.S. management practices.

We will not attempt to interpret the significance of the letters themselves. That should emerge in the comparative study which follows in the next part. In the end, it is hoped each reader will find his or her own meaning and draw conclusions within the context of the book as a whole.

A Letter from Mr. Smith

John Smith was the general manager of a large plant of a U.S. multinational firm located in the western part of the U.S. This firm also owned a plant in Mexico that had in recent years been showing a severe profit slippage. Since the plant Smith had managed in the U.S. had a record of outstanding growth, productivity, and profitability, the head office decided to assign him to manage the Mexican plant in an effort to turn it around. They seemed confident that Mr. Smith had the right qualifications to whip the plant into shape and would use his strength as a hard-nosed manager to good advantage.

Smith was pleased with the promotion and looked forward to the challenge. His only knowledge of Mexico came from a friend who had worked there briefly and had commented on how lazy and undisciplined the Mexicans were. Smith thought this problem could easily be solved and felt that the Mexicans would be grateful for the privilege of having a U.S. executive show them the tricks of the trade. After reviewing the reports in the head office, Smith soon discovered the main problems to be productivity and control, and he began formulating new procedures and controls for the key areas. On arrival in Mexico he began immediately to implement these procedures.

The letter which follows was written six months after Smith began his assignment. In it he relates his initial impressions and experiences to a friend and colleague, Bob Wright, who is on his first assignment abroad in Manila.

Dear Bob,

Now that I have been in Mexico for six months, I thought it was about time to drop you a note and let you know how things are going. Unfortunately, "Not good" is about the best I can say, though things didn't start off too badly. On my first day the finance manager, Mr. González, greeted me in English, and I found him very knowledgeable and friendly. He also seemed amenable to my outline of new control procedures, so I decided immediately to use him as my interpreter.

From my office I noticed that it was well past 9:00 A.M. before the office staff arrived, although working hours were 9:00 to 6:00. So I made a note to add "punctuality" to the agenda for the first staff meeting, which was scheduled for a little later in the morning. At that meeting González first introduced the managers from production, sales, and personnel, each of whom gave me a vigorous handshake. They all appeared very cooperative and expressed their desire to work closely with me. I then reviewed their overall responsibilities as managers and went on to outline my new production and control procedures. Afterwards, I toured the plant with the production manager and González, who pointed out some of the most pressing problems. They both seemed overly anxious for me to meet the key plant supervisors, but I felt there were more important matters to deal with first. Both appeared somewhat disappointed but made no further comment. The remainder of that first day I spent poring over reports that had been left by my predecessor.

During the next few weeks I was rather surprised to find myself bombarded with problems from my managers who, instead of solving the problems themselves, wanted my advice or, worse, wanted me to make their decisions for them. I didn't want to come down too hard on them, since I'd been there only a short time, but I did want to make it clear that I would expect them to handle their responsibilities essentially by themselves in the future—which I did at a meeting called specifically for that purpose.

However, things seemed to go from bad to worse. One day I was on a routine tour of the plant when I encountered a supervisor demonstrating to a worker a procedure which was completely incorrect and would have resulted in a faulty product. Naturally, I wanted to nip the error in the bud, so I immediately pointed out what was wrong and reprimanded the supervisor. The other workers seemed to enjoy the show because they all stopped their work to watch. Afterwards, I summoned the production manager to my office and sternly pointed out his responsibility for the performance of his supervisors and workers and warned that I would not accept a repetition of this incident. The next day the supervisor involved was absent because of illness and the production manager avoided me. I guess I must have made quite an impression. I wanted to set the record straight from the beginning so that they would know I accept no nonsense.

When the problems in the areas of punctuality, hours of work, relief periods and "chatting time" continued, I sent out individual notices of our basic personnel regulations to each employee. In spite of this I have observed only slight improvement in punctuality, so it looks like I'll have to crack down harder.

But personnel problems aren't the only ones I've had to contend with. Last month we had a lot of trouble extracting some machinery from the central customs depot. They wanted more and more details before releasing the goods. González suggested that making a small payment to the customs officer would facilitate the machinery's release and said that the delay was actually caused by the fact that we had not already done so. Of course, I wasn't about to accept that nonsense; blackmail and bribery are not my way of doing business. So I personally took the problem in hand. Alas, to make a long story short, following an unsavory experience, we finally had to pay or they would never have released the goods. Can you believe it!

Next came the problem of one of our telephone lines not functioning. It was urgent because our two remaining lines were constantly occupied. Despite repeated calls and repeated promises that a repairman would arrive "mañana" and despite my personal complaint to the repair service manager, it took one month to get the telephone repaired. It's no wonder I'm getting an ulcer.

After three months in Mexico, I decided to try a different tactic with the managers in our regular weekly meeting, so I announced that we would have a more U.S.-style meeting. You know, a strictly informal, loosen-the-tie and feet-up-on-the-desk type. But instead of relaxing and enjoying the informality, the managers appeared embarrassed, though they didn't comment. I swear, Bob, I don't understand these people. Anyway, following a short pause, the meeting turned to business topics. The big push was still productivity, and we proceeded to lay down the basic outline for a new, integrated procedural program. It was decided that each manager would provide the backup material, put it together in a presentable format, and have it ready for my approval in ten days. About two weeks later each manager presented me with a beautifully laid-out document which contained all the basic concepts we had discussed previously. It was an impressive presentation and they all received well-deserved compliments for a fine job. The details of practical implementation were not discussed because I wanted to leave that up to them. Finally, I felt I was on the right track.

Three weeks later I decided to check on their progress but, Bob, in only one section had the manager even attempted to implement the new program. It was incredible! I immediately summoned the managers to my office and demanded an explanation. The finance manager explained that they were all waiting for my instructions regarding a commencement date. Do I have to spell out everything for these people?

Following that incident I have been very specific in giving instructions, and on the whole the managers seem more productive. But I just don't understand their mentality. Aren't they aware that constant referral to me for decisions and advice reflects on their competence or that accountability is an essential part of their responsibility? Another thing I don't understand is why they always seem so excessively cooperative and agreeable. They rarely make any comments on my decisions unless I specifically request them, and even then the response is very diplomatic and guarded.

Or see if you can figure this one out. Recently I learned about a job opening for a senior sales manager in northern Mexico. I thought of our sales manager, who is very competent, but when I told him about the position, which would be a major step up for him, he showed no interest whatsoever. He politely refused to consider the offer, explaining that his family and his home were here and he was happy, so he had no desire to go elsewhere. Amazing, isn't it? How could he turn down an opportunity for a promotion and a substantial salary increase simply because he liked where he was? No wonder they don't progress!

A few weeks ago I found a striking error in the weekly production report, so I called the production manager to my office. He began to recite a long series of explanations about how the error probably slipped through, but by that time my patience for excuses and wasted time had run out. I interrupted his dissertation and warned him that a repetition of this type of error would not be acceptable. He was obviously embarrassed but stopped making excuses for his actions. To clear the air, I pointed out that

I was criticizing his work, not him personally. He still seemed upset, but I hoped he would get my point.

A different type of situation occurred shortly after that. We were in the process of redecorating the general office when I noticed that the sales manager's office was also in a rather shabby state, so I requested the decorating firm to do it as well. Immediately, I was confronted by the other managers requesting similar treatment for their offices. They protested the implied discrimination and asked if I did not consider their positions in the company of equal importance to that of the sales manager. I assured them that a repainted office was in no way related to the importance of their positions, but they wouldn't let up until I agreed to have all their offices done, even though they really did not need it. I just don't understand their thinking. You'd think a good salary would be a better form of recognition than an unnecessarily repainted office.

Another troublesome incident occurred recently. Following performance reviews, I decided to discharge a number of employees whom I considered "dead wood." Well, I soon discovered that terminations because of incompetence are extremely difficult and costly here in Mexico. We finally managed to dispose of three people, though it wasn't easy, especially since they were relatives of other employees working in the plant. They were very upset! It seems that Mexicans expect their relatives to get hiring and job security preference irrespective of their performance.

Enough of that, I thought, so I issued an order requiring that people be hired on the basis of qualifications and that no preference be given to family or friends. But all this created such a commotion that the union leader came to me and threatened to call a strike, although after his initial protest he seemed to lose interest in hiring and firing issues and shifted his attention to the upcoming union contract renewal. Our company proposals were ready, and I was prepared to discuss our preliminary position, but he didn't seem to have any interest in that either. González told me that it was customary to come to an under-the-table arrangement with the union leader in order to facilitate a quick and problem-free contract. Back where I come from we call this a bribe! I don't play that kind of ball with company principles. However, following a two-day strike and with the threat of more to come, I had no choice but to give in. Since then we have had no further union problems, but I'm still amazed at their approach to labor relations.

Following these problems, I decided to upgrade some basic supervisory skills, so the personnel manager, under my guidance, produced a supervisor's training package. He was worried that some of the supervisors might have trouble understanding the material, so I decided to attend the first training session. After a commendable theoretical presentation by the personnel manager, I tried to get the supervisors to participate in the discussion of implementation of techniques. At that point, the training session came to a grinding halt. No one seemed to know what to say or do. Afterwards, the personnel manager told me that some of the supervisors had only six years of schooling, and as for the personnel manager himself, he seemed unable to convert his theoretical concepts into practical action. This particular problem appears to be common to the whole managerial group, though how you can be a manager without being able to translate theory into action is beyond me.

Speaking of not understanding, it seems that here, family and friends are very much involved in helping each other, even in business. We had an interesting example of this not long ago. We needed some special metal storage shelving in the plant, so I requested the production manager to do a price comparison from two well-known firms in the city, which he did. However, he suggested that a good friend of his could provide it directly from the factory at a favorable price. Interestingly enough, his friend did in fact offer a more favorable price and we accepted it. A similar situation arose with the decorating contract where González suggested contacting his cousin who was in the decorating business. Once again the results were satisfactory. A lot of people in the States would cast a pretty suspicious eye on this kind of mixing of business and personal relations, especially if you ever decided to run for political office!

And then there are production deadlines. For two months I've had a big push on for meeting deadlines. They don't even seem to understand the meaning of a deadline. I sometimes wonder if they will ever learn the basics of efficient management.

Overall, as you can see, these past six months have been extremely frustrating. Although the Mexicans are courteous and unquestioning in their acceptance of my authority, they just silently ignore aspects of their work they either don't understand or don't agree with. What a mentality to try to decipher! Nevertheless, in spite of my frustrations, I still feel that tight controls and a strict approach are the only ways to teach them the right way to run a business.

Naturally, the language barrier is still a problem, but with González as interpreter and only another two years to go, it seems hardly worthwhile wasting time studying Spanish. It certainly won't be of much use at home. Joanne is finding life in Mexico extremely frustrating as well. Thank goodness we live in an area of the city where there are a lot of other Americans with whom we can let down our hair and compare notes. It's consoling to find that everyone else has the same problems we do with the Mexican mentality. Fortunately, after my assignment here is finished, this plant becomes someone else's headache, and I shall be very content to return home to a situation I understand.

But enough. What I have written represents only a sampling of what has happened so far. I could go on and on, but I won't. I hope your assignment in Manila is proving more rewarding than mine. Drop me a line when you have a minute.

Cordially,

John

A Letter from Sr. González

Sr. González is Mr. Smith's finance manager and interpreter. The following is a letter written by Sr. González to his friend and colleague, Pablo, who holds an executive post in a Mexican company located in another city.

Dear Pablo,

I hope this letter finds you and your delightful family in good health and spirits and you are continuing to enjoy life in your beautiful city. As for us, we are all well, but I continue to be very disillusioned with my work. As you have asked on many occasions, I have finally put aside some time to relate to you some of my views and experiences with this U.S. company.

First, I must point out that I have great admiration for the technological knowledge and administrative skills of the North Americans. Undoubtedly, these two factors have contributed greatly to their tremendous development and business success. However, when they attempt to impose their methods on us, huge problems arise, and we all feel frustrated and resentful but don't know what to do about it.

In my experience, the U.S. executive seems to be a cold, impersonal, discourteous, and critical individual. His main objective appears to be to dehumanize business as much as possible and to convert people into robots. He seems to think we should "live to work" and enjoy life only if there is time. Friends and family are secondary and should never be discussed at work. Can you imagine! What a boring life he must have.

When Mr. Smith first arrived here, he had absolutely no knowledge of Mexico or our customs. He assumed that U.S. methods could be introduced directly, without modifications, and that efficiency would result if sufficient pressure were exerted in order to achieve conformity. He did not realize that he was asking us to change customs which have existed for hundreds of years and are deeply embedded in all Mexicans. People can't just suddenly change the way they have been doing things all their lives. It seems to me that an adaptation of the U.S. system is necessary so we can benefit from their technological achievements and organizational know-how, but we should do so without sacrificing our traditions.

Unfortunately, Mr. Smith seems to believe that we are all just dying to embrace "the American way." He is convinced of its superiority and openly expresses this belief. What a problem it is to try to convince someone with such a conceited attitude that his approach simply won't work here!

In order to give you an idea of how this attitude has affected our working lives, I will give you a few examples.

On our first day with Mr. Smith as general manager, I welcomed him and introduced him to the other managers. He shook hands (though without much enthusiasm) but refused to take the time or make the effort to meet the key plant supervisors. You can well imagine the hurt feelings. However, Mr. Smith appeared unaware not only of the negative reactions caused by his neglect, but, in general, of the necessity for extending basic courtesies and consideration for other people and of the importance of this in maintaining the respect of his subordinates.

He seems, in addition, to feel that all errors require instant criticism and are mostly inexcusable. He said once that personal feelings are not important and that we must learn to overcome our sensitivity to criticism. We couldn't believe what we heard! Shortly after his arrival he severely criticized a supervisor on the plant floor in the presence of all the workers. The supervisor involved was naturally most embarrassed and distressed, even to the point of pleading illness for the following two days. His respect for Mr. Smith has understandably been permanently damaged, and his general attitude toward his work has suffered as a result of the incident.

On another occasion the production manager was summoned to Mr. Smith's office, and, with myself as interpreter, he also received a harsh rebuke for an error in the weekly production figures. Mr. Smith showed no patience or understanding when the production manager attempted to give a reasonable explanation for the occurrence. For me, naturally, the whole episode was extremely embarrassing, but fortunately the production manager and I are good friends, so it has led to no hard feelings between us. In addition to these examples many smaller incidents have occurred, and in fact the only conversation which takes place between Mr. Smith and the managers, or any staff member, involves some aspect of work. He seems to look for reasons to criticize instead of praise—something we hear very little of.

As an example of Mr. Smith's attempts to turn us all into robots, let me explain his views about time. To him, time is top priority in every aspect of our working life. He once said, "Time is money," so we shouldn't waste any of it. Therefore, he has endeavored to enforce strict regulations on punctuality, rest periods, and hours of work. On the other hand, he gives little or no recognition to those of us who work late without complaint, nor does he have any patience with staff members who have legitimate problems of punctuality, such as erratic public transportation. All he does is make the controls even tighter for every infraction of the regulations. He is obsessed with deadlines and treats them as if they were oaths. These methods have created a tense and disagreeable atmosphere, which has proven detrimental rather than beneficial to overall productivity.

To compound this situation, we have just survived a potentially dangerous episode involving Mr. Smith's decision to terminate three employees. We expressed our concern but he was adamant, and when the union leader arrived, he even resisted paying the commission which the union leader expected. It took the threat of a long strike (the workers did go off for two days) before he learned that in Mexico negotiating with a union is sometimes done differently from the way it is done in the U.S. and finally agreed to compensate the union leader. As a result we now have a new contract, but the plant has not returned to normal. Since Mr. Smith decided to virtually prohibit the hiring of relatives of staff members, there has been general dissatisfaction and even a number of resignations. We hope we can convince him to drop these regulations or there will be no end to the friction.

Another problem came up when we tried to get the equipment out of customs. You can imagine how Mr. Smith reacted when the customs officer kept delaying and asking for more and more papers—obviously wanting some small tip for his efforts (a bribe, in other words). The whole situation could have been solved very easily and inexpensively if Mr. Smith had listened to us and accepted that we know best how to handle these situations in Mexico.

On the whole, it appears Mr. Smith has little sensitivity to the human relations aspects of management. Perhaps this would not be compatible with his objective of turning us into robots. Yet, how can you take the human element out of the workplace? Surely he must know that productivity depends on motivated and happy people. Mr. Smith is obviously missing the point if he regards us as machines to be manipulated rather than human beings to be respected and motivated.

Another thing we don't understand (or like) is his approach to the delegation of authority. He apparently assumes that we are all equally accustomed to accepting complete responsibility for our own areas, to the point where any mistakes or shortcomings on the part of any staff member result in his criticizing us severely, even in front of staff and colleagues. I would very much like to have full authority for my own area because this is what my training led me to expect, but I cannot accept his undiplomatic handling of the inevitable occasional mistakes that occur. Also, the older managers cling to our tradition of leaving all authority and decision making in the hands of the general manager, so they refer all problems to him. For those of us who would like to assume more responsibility and authority, this situation results in considerable frustration. However, none of us managers feels any confidence in Mr. Smith's tact in handling problems. If he continues in his present fashion, we shall all be made to look foolish in front of our subordinates and colleagues.

On a more personal note, none of us envies him his lifestyle, which seems to involve nothing but work, with very little time for leisure. We have never met his wife or family, and he never mentions them. It certainly must be a strange existence. After all, what is life worth if one does not have time to enjoy it with family and friends?

Finally, though I mentioned this before, there is the question of good manners. Most North Americans are apparently unaware of the unfortunate impression they create when they disregard common courtesies. In addition to the incident that occurred on the day of his arrival, let me tell you another story—the ultimate example of bad manners! One day he called a "U.S.-style informal meeting." He actually put his feet up on top of the desk. Can you imagine a Mexican general manager behaving in such an uncivilized fashion? However, Mr. Smith seemed completely unaware of the reason for our embarrassment, and of course we couldn't comment. How could he be so inconsiderate?

Mr. Smith is very abrupt in his approach to people in general, without any concept of courtesy when requesting information or questioning procedures, sometimes forgetting to say "please" and "thank you" when dealing with his staff. It seems he has no time for us. He always seems preoccupied with work and maybe forgets that these small courtesies are important. He never asks about our families or our health—unless it interferes with our work efficiency.

Pablo, this letter has ended up being a long list of complaints and criticisms. I guess I needed to express how I feel. Anyway, I hope some of this will be useful to you when you go to that management conference in Dallas next month. Perhaps you will have a more favorable impression of American managers there.

My warmest greetings to your family, and I look forward to your reply.

Fondest regards,

Luís

Part II

Comparative Study

What lies behind the dramatic differences and major misunderstandings that John and Luís write about? Here we will look for an answer in a comparative study which analyzes not only the differing cultural factors which affect management styles in Mexico and the United States, but also those aspects of management style which are particularly sensitive to cultural variations. In this way it is hoped that the reader will be able to appreciate the considerable contrasts which exist and to recognize more readily the causes of cross-cultural management problems when they arise. The basic issue in cross-cultural management is summarized perceptively by Massie and Lutyes (1972), who suggest that U.S. management approaches have spread to other countries in part because these are the techniques used throughout the world by U.S. companies, and in part because the early recognition and development of business education by U.S. universities made the United States a leader in this field. However, difficulties have arisen, and "the problem is quite similar to that of transplanting an organ in the medical field: a healthy organ may function nicely in its home environment (the original body), but be rejected, or unable to function properly in the body of the recipient" (7).

Harris and Moran, in their book *Managing Cultural Differences* (1986), stress that a person "should realize that his or her knowledge and perception are valid only for self and not for the rest of the world" (53). With these perspectives in mind, let us turn to the specifics of culture and management style that are central to effectiveness in the cross-cultural workplace.

But first a word about the nature of the study. Based as it is on interviews with Mexican and U.S. executives, it was almost inevitable that the value judgments of the interviews would infiltrate the text to some degree. The author has made every effort to eliminate or neutralize them where they appeared.

A greater problem lay in the emergence of stereotypes. Not only were they embodied in the commentary of the interviewees, they are almost inescapable when one makes generalizations about culture. Yet no generalization or stereotype regarding cultural characteristics can apply to every member of a cultural group.

The author owes much to psychologist Edward C. Stewart for a way out of this dilemma (see *American Cultural Patterns: A Cross-Cultural Perspective*, rev. ed., Stewart and Bennett). Stewart divides cultural assumptions and values into four major components:

1. Form of activity

2. Form of social relations

3. Perception of the world

4. Perception of self and of the individual

Within each of these categories he identifies a variety of ways that human beings think and behave and major differences in what they value and in what assumptions they make. Under "form of activity," for example, Stewart notes that Americans are oriented toward *doing*. Getting things done is a virtue on which most Americans place a high value. In other cultures a higher value may be placed on *being*, which emphasizes the intrinsic quality of the individual. It is Stewart's argument (elaborated by David Hoopes 1979) that in any group or culture virtually every kind of value orientation—including those which are diametrically opposed—can be found, but that some will predominate. Those particular values and traits will then be seen to characterize that culture and seem typical, even though different contrasting values may be quite strong. This concept is referred to as *preponderance of belief* (26).

As an example, in the United States business executives tend to rank work above family on their scale of priorities. For them, work considerations come first and family considerations are made to fit in around them. The Mexican executive, on the other hand, tends to rank family above work on his priority scale. This does not mean that in either group there are not many individuals who depart from these norms, only that one value tends to be predominant. Stewart illustrates the concept

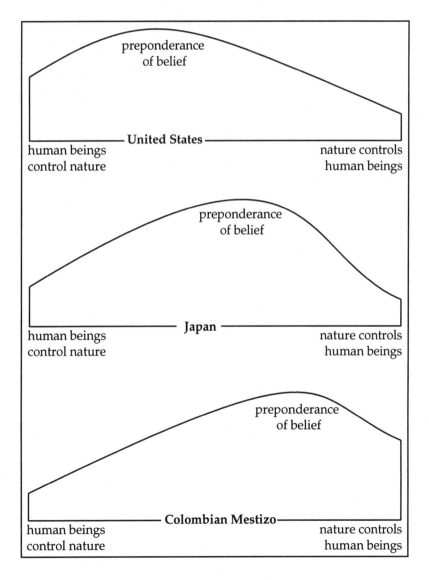

by means of a diagram of frequency distribution, where the position of the peak indicates the preponderance of belief. It clearly illustrates the relative nature of preponderance of belief and the existence of many individuals who do not conform to it.

Generalizations about a culture and the people who share it are based on the preponderance of a certain set of characteristics. The author recognizes that these generalizations may appear to stereotype Mexicans and Americans, who are the subject of this book. But the generalizations are necessary if the book is going to be of practical value. Our aim here is not to analyze and dissect culture but to observe as objectively as possible how culture is embodied in and influences behavior. Generalizations, though superficial in some sense, provide a valuable tool for understanding why people behave the way they do. Thus, if this is going to be a handbook of cross-cultural management for the busy executive, we want to examine culture not for its own sake, but as it throws light on everyday behavior. Further, brevity is called for. Not all aspects of culture are covered, only those that bear significantly on the cross-cultural interaction of the two groups. Much is left out, but the result is greater focus and economy and, ultimately, the more satisfactory accomplishment of the aims of this book.

The comparative study is divided into two sections. In the first of these, the cultural and personal traits of U.S. and Mexican executives are compared:

—Family	—Etiquette
—Religion	—Personal Appearance
—Education	—Status
—Nationalism	—Aesthetics
—Personal Sensitivity	—Ethics

The second section similarly compares the most important aspects of their management styles:

—Work/Leisure	—Loyalty
—Direction/Supervision	—Competition
—Theory versus Practice	—Training and Development
—Control	—Time
—Staffing	—Planning

Cultural Traits

FAMILY ──

Mexico

The traditional family is still the foundation of Mexican society. Family takes precedence over work and all other aspects of life. As one Mexican executive said, "Our family is our first priority and must remain so for the future stability of our country." Within the family unit, the father is the undisputed authority figure. All major decisions are made by him, and he sets the disciplinary standards. The mother is subservient and seeks the advice and authority of her husband in all major matters. She is expected to be a devoted mother and obedient wife and is revered as such. The Mexican executive's wife has not usually worked outside the home before marriage and has little knowledge or understanding of her husband's work. Gradually, however, young wives are working more professionally and their subservient role is slowly changing. Their two worlds meet, however, in their dedication to the family, and especially to their children. Children are protected and loved. They are accepted and enjoyed, and the normal weekend recreation consists of entire family units, including a variety of relatives and friends, visiting each other or going out together. Growing up in these circumstances, children feel secure but are very dependent on the moral support of their families. Likewise, children respect their parents and grandparents and care for them in their old age.

Upon reaching school age and having been conditioned by the home environment, the child tends to accept school discipline as an extension of parental discipline. This does not necessarily mean that the children are all well-behaved, but their resistance to discipline is often clothed in deviousness rather than overt rebellion, a trait sometimes carried into adulthood. The child usually becomes a conformist, accepting the rigidity of the school system in which the teacher is the undisputed authority and in which the development of a questioning mind is inhibited.

As a result of his upbringing and education, a young executive appears obsequious to his superior and accepts instructions unquestioningly. He is unaccustomed to solving problems that arise and feels little sense of personal accountability. Since all authority resides in his superior, the subordinate's responsibility is limited to carrying out instructions.

In addition, because of his strong emotional attachment to family and friends, there is considerable resistance to moving away from them; the need for that attachment and support is simply too strong. The Mexican executive is therefore not as mobile as his U.S. counterpart and will not happily move to another city, let alone to another country (though Mexicans of course do move when economic necessity forces it).

United States

Work has a high priority in the United States, and the family is expected to fit in around work requirements. Families are also expected to be mobile, moving frequently during their working lives. As a result, the family unit tends to consist of father, mother, and children who, in most cases, have very little contact with other relatives. Many children see little of their parents, especially if they both work. In addition to this situation, the concept of the "one-parent family" has taken hold in the United States, placing additional burdens on the single parent who now has even less time available for the children because of the necessity of working full-time. The current family situation has created a great deal of controversy, because of the accompanying loss of traditional family values.

Within the family unit, the father is not normally regarded as the sole wielder of authority; this is shared with the mother.

This kind of family structure fosters in the children self-sufficiency, independence, and individualism—qualities much admired in the United States. It also results in children being almost as heavily influenced by peers as by their parents. Strong family attachments and dependencies tend to be severed at quite an early age. Most young people are considered ready to live away from home by the time they are of university age, and they enjoy the independence and freedom it gives them in making their own decisions.

For the most part, young people dislike being told what to do and prefer to cope with their own problems rather than to seek advice from their parents, teachers, or some other older person. This attitude may cause conflict within the family, and it carries over into adulthood, manifesting itself as a readiness to criticize and to attempt to change what one disagrees with in society in general. As one executive put it, "We are not as ready to take things as they are if we feel these things are wrong." On the other hand, young people, for the most part, accept the standards and laws which protect their community. It should also be noted that in recent years some of the rebelliousness of the 1960s has abated. There is a trend now toward greater acceptance of establishment values, even though these are also beginning to be questioned in the new concern over long-term environmental and lifestyle issues. As a result of home and school conditioning, the young U.S. graduate still arrives in a business organization full of self-confidence and with most of the desired qualities—independence, competitiveness, aggressiveness, and individualism.

When the executive moves to a new location—either because the company requires it or for career advancement—the contact with the extended family is further weakened. Frequent relocation also makes it difficult to maintain lasting friendships and to establish solid roots in a community. Moving to another country adds a further dimension. For most executives, it will be the first time in their lives that they have to deal with a significantly different environment—a new language, strange customs, people who think differently from themselves. It will be their first encounter with the kind of disorientation people experience when working abroad. In these circumstances, the family unit is drawn closely together, and its members become very dependent on one another for moral support. Therefore, harmony within the family unit becomes a crucial factor in the happiness and success of executives on foreign assignment. It is also natural for them to seek out other expatriates who share their background and with whom they can communicate. What results is the formation of American ghettos which keep the expatriates from reaching out and making contact with local people. As one Mexican executive said, "With so many Americans living a ghetto existence and associating only with other Americans, how can they ever get to know what makes us tick?"

RELIGION

Mexico

The Roman Catholic church is deeply rooted in Mexican history, and about 90 percent of the country's population is Roman Catholic. This does not mean that all Mexicans are regular churchgoers or particularly devout. Most, however, observe the basic rituals of the church, such as baptisms, first communions, marriages, and funerals. Within the family it is mainly the mother who looks after the children's religious preparation and upbringing.

The business community generally sees religion as a positive, cohesive force, and many factories and offices display religious images in prominent places, the most revered being the Virgin of Guadalupe. It is also customary to have new premises blessed by a priest, and on special occasions masses may be said on the premises for employees and their families. It is felt that this practice makes a valuable contribution to staff morale. A few companies have a policy of hiring only Roman Catholics to avoid religious conflict among employees, but this is rare. There are also companies in which religion plays no visible part.

In addition to this acceptance of formal religious practices, there is a mysticism which pervades much of Mexican thinking. Many Mexicans feel that their lives are controlled by a Higher Power, so that they can fatalistically accept success or failure, happiness or tragedy, wealth or poverty. While such an attitude provides them with resilience in bad times, it also, particularly in the lower echelons of society, inclines them to accept whatever is, discouraging effort and initiative. In work situations U.S. executives often interpret this as laziness.

United States

The people of the United States come from varied religious backgrounds, predominantly Protestant, though there are large numbers of Catholics in the United States. Most respect, if not share, the Protestant ethic in which honesty, integrity, hard work, and diligence are highly valued. Generally, children have some religious preparation, and (if Christian) many go to Sunday school during their early years, though vast numbers do not. During adolescence they normally experience little pressure from their parents for religious conformity, though in the end most follow their parents' faith.

Because religion is so personal in the United States and because almost everyone believes strongly in the separation of church and state (as is required in the U.S. Constitution), U.S. society appears quite secular, with little open manifestation of religion, and religion is virtually never brought into the workplace.

EDUCATION ─────────────────────

Mexico

Mexican pedagogy is based on traditional French and Spanish patterns of deductive reasoning, moving from the general to the particular, from the abstract to the concrete. In practice this translates into the rote learning of abstract concepts, usually long before they can be understood. Ideas and concepts are introduced in early primary grades, and children are required to memorize them and reproduce them verbatim for examinations on which all grading is based. Little credit is given for classroom work; students therefore become very examination-oriented. As a student progresses through high school to the university, the method remains basically the same, though the concepts are better understood and are related to concrete reality as students become more and more intellectually sophisticated. But the next step, learning how to apply ideas in practical situations, is hardly ever taken. It is not surprising, then, that Mexicans often have difficulty developing the problem-solving skills essential in the workplace.

Students generally accept the rigid conformity demanded by the school system, in part probably because of their exposure to an authoritarian father figure during childhood. Children with quick and inquisitive minds are pressured into conformity. Original thinking is discouraged, and students of above average intelligence generally either lapse into boredom and become lazy or possibly rebel in subtle ways.

Great importance is attached to the attractive presentation of student work, to the point that it is sometimes valued as highly as the quality of the content. As regards subject matter, emphasis is placed on the acquisition of general knowledge in subjects such as world geography and history, sociology, literature, languages, and the basics of the natural sciences. A person with this breadth of knowledge, combined with the good breeding that is the norm in upper-class families, is considered a "cultured person" *(una persona muy culta)* and is highly esteemed. Thus, the average university graduate arrives in the business world with a good grounding in general knowledge and an interest in the world at large, but may lack depth in his field of specialization.

United States

The U.S. pedagogical approach is pragmatic and concrete in contrast to the Mexican. Great stress is laid on the development of analytical skills, and subjects are related to concrete situations as much as possible. Instead of rote learning, the emphasis is on understanding underlying concepts and their application. The amassing of knowledge per se is generally not encouraged. There is a strong feeling that only "usable" knowledge is worth having.

In the United States the educational orientation is strongly U.S.-centered, so that a college graduate often has little knowledge of the rest of the world. Specialization comes early, so students acquire a significant depth of knowledge but in a comparatively narrow field. This is consistent with the emphasis on "useful" knowledge, since a certain depth of understanding is necessary before knowledge can be put into practice.

Discipline is relatively lax at most elementary and secondary schools, and students enjoy considerable freedom of expression. Teachers are generally punctual and conscientious in their work and observe the ethical norms expected of them. Any breach of ethics by teacher or student is severely punished.

College faculty are highly qualified, disciplined, and mostly conscientious. Young graduates are usually competent in their fields but are often limited in other interests. Their breadth of knowledge may seem quite narrow as regards things outside their own country. For this reason they are often perceived as being relatively parochial or unsophisticated as compared to young adults in other countries regarding subjects of general interest.

NATIONALISM

Mexico

Most Mexicans are intensely patriotic, nationalistic, and usually very proud of their regional identities. They feel great pride in their country's long history, traditions, and culture and are ready to verbalize their feelings at every opportunity. Throughout their early upbringing and school life, this pride is instilled in them. The importance attached to continuity of tradition is evident both in social activities and in the workplace, and there is a growing concern over the influence of the consumer society and its intrusion into the traditional value system. While desiring to assimilate modern technological developments and to modernize their economy, most Mexicans want to maintain their traditions and basic values.

With their deep attachment to their country, Mexicans have little desire to live anywhere else. Nevertheless, the difficult economic situation at home has for generations obliged Mexicans to seek work in the United States or in the border regions.

Mexican nationalism has caused some foreign companies to have misgivings about putting Mexicans in senior executive positions, fearing that it might outweigh loyalty to the company should a conflict of loyalties arise. This concern is evidently not universal, since a growing number of foreign organizations are appointing Mexicans to top positions.

United States

Citizens of the United States are also nationalistic, though they would be more inclined to call themselves "patriotic." In the United States this patriotic impulse focuses especially on the ideals embodied in the Declaration of Independence, the Constitution, and other historic documents and statements, such as the Gettysburg Address.

Above all, Americans are proud of the vastness and wealth of their country. They are fully convinced that, given a chance, everyone would like to be a citizen of the United States, to have what they have, do as they do and, once properly educated, think as they think. They are convinced of the superiority of the "American way of life" and find it inconceivable that anybody might choose to live differently. The resulting attitude of superiority has, not surprisingly, caused a great deal of animosity abroad, especially when openly voiced.

PERSONAL SENSITIVITY —————————————————

Mexico

Mexicans are extremely sensitive to the world around them and have a marked capacity to empathize with the people with whom they interact. They also tend to be agile diplomats, skilled at avoiding confrontation and loss of face. In potentially confrontational situations they strive to reach a consensus, where there are no outright winners or losers. They are also highly sensitive to criticism because of a deep emotional response to everything which affects them personally (this includes criticism of their work, which is taken as personal). For this reason they try to avoid situations which show them in a negative light or involve them in conflict. Because of this sensitivity, non-Mexicans often consider Mexicans "thin-skinned" or victims of an inferiority complex. Such an interpretation, however, misses the importance of saving face in a close-knit society, where one's standing with friends and colleagues is at stake. As one Mexican executive told the author, "You cannot criticize a Mexican in front of his friends. It is a disgrace, and he will hate you for the rest of his life."

Face-saving practices, however, are so deeply ingrained and instinctive that they are sometimes engaged in even when not strictly necessary and result in the elaborate excuses and white lies one often hears.

United States

Quite apart from the "stiff upper lip" attitude which is so much a part of Anglo-Saxon culture, the rough-and-tumble of the business world obliges U.S. executives to suppress any sensitivity they may have. From early youth, U.S. males are conditioned to hide emotions, as any emotional display is regarded as a sign of weakness. Toughness and a hard-nosed attitude are qualities which are respected and admired. It is generally understood that emotions and business do not mix; this enables U.S. managers to accept criticism of their work and to profit from that criticism by improving their professional performance, without taking it personally. As aptly stated by one executive, "Remember, in business we criticize your work, we do not criticize you personally."

Examples of this thick-skinned attitude are evident in every working day. A superior may reprimand a subordinate quite sternly for an error he or she has committed, but a few minutes later the two may be found laughing together over a cup of coffee. Or managers may express conflicting views at a meeting, giving rise to heated discussion. However, the meeting over, all is forgotten and their personal relations are as amicable as ever. It is often felt that a solution arrived at after a lively discussion is more likely to be well-analyzed and thought-out than one made without dissenting opinions being voiced. In short, emotions are considered to be personal, with no place in the tough world of business.

On the other hand, outside the work situation Americans are liable to be as emotionally sensitive as anyone else. This becomes evident whenever a foreigner questions or criticizes any aspect of the "American way of life." As much as, and possibly even more than, people in most other countries, average American businesspeople have become so conditioned to feeling superior that they find it inconceivable that anyone could call into question their fundamental beliefs, their ways of thinking or doing things. A response often heard is, "If you don't like it here, you better go back to where you came from."

ETIQUETTE

Mexico

Mexicans, at all social levels, attach great importance to courtesy in social intercourse. While the actual code of conduct varies from one social milieu to another, good manners are always recognized as a sign of breeding. A well-mannered person is described as *muy educado*, the connotation being that manners are inculcated during the educational process. Both at home and at school a child is taught polite forms of greeting and leave-taking, respect for elders, and consideration for smaller children. Failure to conform to the norms of polite behavior stamps a person as rude, disrespectful, and generally ill-bred *(mal educado)*. On first meeting people, Mexicans will immediately evaluate their manners. If they measure up, the Mexicans will respect them and feel at ease with them. If they do not, they will have as little as possible to do with them.

In the business environment, there is an etiquette, a certain set of expected behaviors, which is followed. These behaviors include ritual handshaking and greeting of staff in the morning upon arrival at work. Some convivial remark must always accompany a greeting, such as asking after the person's health and/or family. These polite forms are also necessary in meetings, on the telephone, in conversation (even when voicing a complaint or disagreement), in restaurants and public places. "Please" and "thank you" with a smile are seldom forgotten, and courtesy in correspondence is carried to great lengths.

Etiquette also governs the use of first names and the two forms of "you": *usted* (formal) and *tu* (familiar). The former is always used in business contacts, except with personal friends. In formal conversation and correspondence, it is polite to address a person by his title, e.g., *Licenciado, Ingeniero*, or *Doctor*.

"Tu" is reserved for those people whom you call by first names, i.e., family and friends. It is a breach of etiquette to use "tu" or first names until the senior person has indicated that it would be in order.

Overall, the Mexican is a warm person, accustomed to close physical contact. When meeting family and friends, men give the women and children a kiss on the cheek and exchange vigorous hugs with other men, accompanied by a pat on the back. This ritual is not followed with strangers or low-ranking subordinates. Instead, a simple handshake is exchanged. By contrast, motorists generally show little courtesy and consideration for other drivers (which makes driving in Mexico a hair-raising experience for North Americans not accustomed to it).

In general then, Mexican executives are courteous and diplomatic and never openly boast of their achievements, which would be considered in bad taste and would make them lose credibility and respect. Etiquette demands a low-key, respectful, and, sometimes, a seemingly obsequious posture.

United States

In business dealings, because time is money and efficiency is of the essence, courtesy and diplomacy are often relegated to second place. U.S. executives want to get straight to the point. They are accustomed to making direct, concise statements, without taking into account the possibility of sensitive reactions on the other side. Since they are conditioned to separating emotions from work and consider time too precious to be wasted, they often show little empathy for others at work and neglect the little courtesies which are needed to create a harmonious atmosphere in the Mexican work environment. This lack of empathy is easily interpreted as bad manners, and thus U.S. executives often find themselves in the awkward position of having offended someone without being aware that they have said or done anything wrong. In many cases, behavior that is considered acceptable in the United States may be considered discourteous or even offensive in Mexico. Executives who have not been properly briefed are likely to commit many a blunder before discovering the customs of the country for themselves.

In many U.S. families little stress is laid on teaching good manners as part of the children's upbringing. Children often appear awkward when introduced to adults or when exposed to situations outside their immediate community, having had little or no guidance on how to behave in these circumstances. As they grow into young adults, they gradually absorb the basic norms of behavior expected in their community. Even so, their intense individualism may at times outweigh any feeling of obligation to be courteous. One may encounter disrespect for the elderly and lack of consideration for children and the handicapped. Fortunately, such behavior is not universal.

In their everyday contact with Mexican executives, most U.S. executives are not accustomed to routinely shaking hands upon saying good morning. Shaking hands is reserved for introductions. Nor do they normally greet staff members, except for the few working in or around their office. As far as their colleagues' or subordinates' state of health (or that of their families) is concerned, those subjects rarely cross their minds. They are usually too fully occupied (or preoccupied) by work and its problems, such as in this example from the experience of one Mexican executive: "I was absent from work for a week because of a severe illness. Upon my return, there was not one comment or question about my health. My boss immediately started talking about business matters, as if I had never been absent."

U.S. executives are in a way paradoxical because away from the office they are for the most part friendly and warm and considerate of family and friends. At work, however, they put on their "business faces," which hide emotion in the interest of greater efficiency, often at the expense of courtesy.

Even the informality and use of first names which prevails in the workplace in the United States do not alter the basic attitude that business is, first and foremost, business.

PERSONAL APPEARANCE

Mexico

Overall physical appearance influences Mexicans considerably in their first impression of a person. When Mexicans describe people they have just met for the first time, their initial comments usually refer to appearance, manners, and personal qualities. Their achievements come second. Good clothes and careful grooming are expected of anyone in a managerial position. Most executives dress with the same old-world formality that characterizes their manners. They know its importance in maintaining the respect of their subordinates. They likewise expect their staff to be well-dressed and well-groomed, certainly at the senior levels. This is very evident in advertisements for employment, where good presentation is often called for, sometimes even before mention is made of the required skills or academic qualifications.

It should be noted in passing that Mexicans in general, not just executives, dress conservatively, even outside work. In the city most women wear dresses or skirts instead of slacks, and men wear long trousers. Shorts are considered beach and sports apparel. Women are increasingly seen in slacks, but seldom wear them in the office. The upper-class Mexican family tends to dress expensively, and careful grooming at all times is considered a status symbol associated with good breeding. A sloppy, unkempt appearance is associated with poor breeding. The Mexican executive is very much affected by the personal appearance of a foreigner, so a first impression can be greatly enhanced by careful grooming.

United States

In the U.S. business community, reasonable grooming is normally required, but ultimately more importance is placed on ability, qualifications, achievements, and performance than on what one looks like. In this action-oriented, informal society, concern with the exterior facade is secondary. The individual tends to choose comfort before fashion, although some companies do have dress regulations which may cover such things as length of hair, beards, and even the type of clothes, since many businesses wish to present a middle-class, establishment image. One thus generally finds that, in the office, executives and office staff wear conservative business clothes. During leisure time or when out shopping, dress tends to be extremely casual. In warm weather, men and women of all ages can be seen on city streets and in shopping centers wearing shorts and beach clothes. Young people live in jeans and casual clothing and generally attach little importance to neatness and grooming. For most people, the quest for comfort outweighs any inclination to be well-groomed in the traditional sense.

STATUS

Mexico

On the Mexican scale of values, status ranks very high. A man who holds an academic degree or a position bearing an impressive title commands great respect and admiration among family, friends, and the community at large. A consequence often deplored by Mexican executives is that too many professional-level people are educated in Mexico as lawyers, doctors, and engineers, and too few as middle-level technicians. Everyone who can possibly get it wants the status a degree gives. The titles of *Licenciado, Doctor,* or *Ingeniero* may not necessarily represent high academic achievement, nor the position of *Director* of a company be the result of great business acumen, but the title confers status on the holder, and lesser mortals hold him in awe.

Many positions are, of course, still obtained through family connections and personal or political influence. Family background, as indicated by paternal and maternal surnames, is a particularly important factor in determining one's standing in the community. The offspring of upper-class families are virtually assured prestigious positions, even though their abilities and performance might be no better than average. On the other hand, children from modest homes may show great ability and potential for achievement, yet find it difficult to gain recognition and rise in the hierarchical structure because they lack the right connections. Thus, in spite of the prestige associated with status and position, one does not necessarily find the best-qualified people in the most responsible positions. The general outlook is well summed up in the comment of a Mexican executive, "If a Mexican has to choose, he will always prefer status to achievement."

United States

Status in U.S. society is based mainly on achievement and, to some degree, its concomitant wealth. In their work, U.S. executives seek opportunities for achievement because they know this will bring recognition and wealth. Wealth and the possession of material goods have become identified with status. But the "idle rich" do not generally have status; the respectable wealthy are admired because of their achievements, not just their wealth. Wealth, therefore, is a symbol of achievement more often than it is a status symbol in itself. The result, on the other hand, is a pervasive and intense focus on the acquisition of material possessions and indulgence in expensive pastimes, such as vacationing in exotic places and joining exclusive clubs. Little importance is attached these days to family background. People rarely ask "Who is your father?" Those older wealthy families which still exist tend to keep a low profile, while the majority of middle-class executives display their wealth proudly.

AESTHETICS

Mexico

Mexicans in general tend to be romantic, mystical, and artistic. One might say that many are dreamers, in the sense of being unrealistic, finding pleasure in the aesthetic aspects of life at the expense of attending to the practical, everyday drudgery of making a living. Mexican business executives are no exception, even though these traits are tempered by their business training and experience.

The aesthetic trait manifests itself in various ways. Starting with school life, much time and effort are spent on the attractive presentation of work, even though the significance of the content is not always understood. In the workplace also, significant importance is still attached to attractive presentation, such as in training programs, where impressive diplomas and certificates are awarded for sometimes insignificant achievements. Long, rhetorical, flowery speeches plus much pomp and ceremony are indulged in at every opportunity. Social occasions would not be complete without music (preferably a folkloric band), decorations, and dancing, all of which require considerable talent and effort to produce.

As to the "dreamer" aspect, Mexican executives have extremely agile minds, with the ability to pursue philosophical ideas with flourish and subtlety and to develop elaborate plans which will be described with great enthusiasm. These presentations are accepted with pleasure and satisfaction among Mexicans. Hardly anyone will question the practicality of the schemes. The question of implementation is not likely even to be raised. As a result, many excellent ideas never come to fruition. As one writer summed it up, "In Latin America, the word is very often a substitute for the deed."

United States

The aesthetic sense of average U.S. executives is not particularly developed. Inclination toward aesthetic pursuits is generally suppressed in favor of activities that are more likely to further their careers. All their energies are concentrated on the business of making money. Therefore, in the workplace, manifestations of aesthetics are largely absent (except perhaps in the executive's plush office—which denotes his status). Any individual executive who is particularly gifted artistically expresses it outside the workplace. This general underdevelopment of artistic perspectives often makes it difficult for executives to work effectively with persons who are essentially creative artists. However, the difficulty may be due to conditioning rather than to basic nature. The U.S. executive is trained to consider business a cold place, where hard logic leaves no room for aesthetic displays. This aspect of the workplace is changing, however. Small businesses especially are demonstrating an increasing aesthetic sensitivity, but this trend is not likely to be apparent in the foreign operations of large corporations.

ETHICS

Mexico

The code of ethics to which the vast majority of Mexicans subscribe is based on Christian morality as preached by the Roman Catholic Church. Most Mexicans deplore the really gross unethical practices they witness daily.

Throughout the educational process the Mexican student is confronted by practices which, while generally considered unethical, are tacitly condoned. During primary school the progress of a child is measured exclusively by government examinations. Consequently, when a student is poorly prepared for the exam, it is not uncommon for the teacher to provide help or let him or her repeat it so as to get satisfactory results. In the higher grades, the practice of using hidden notes *(acordeones)* is common, even though most school authorities deny it and ostensibly punish offenders.

At the university, other abuses are encountered. Since some larger universities have strong political affiliations, a student's active political support almost guarantees a degree and, sometimes, even a political career. By the same token, opposition to the university's political alignment can mean delay of a student's degree or even expulsion. It is not uncommon for professors to be late or absent from classes; examination results are sometimes bought or rigged, and payoffs of professors are not unknown. Fortunately, these abuses are not universal, and there are a large number of conscientious, dedicated, and highly principled professors who command the respect of the students. Most students deplore these abuses and are quick to distinguish between good and poor teaching and high and low ethical standards. Some university authorities have also made valiant efforts to eradicate, or at least curtail, these practices.

With this background, young Mexican executives arrive in the business world—some with their professional ethics permanently marred, while others, repelled by what they have seen, insist on maintaining high personal and professional standards.

The aspect of ethics most discussed and written about on both sides of the border is undoubtedly that of corruption. Since this has been so well covered, albeit tendentiously at times, it is sufficient for the purposes of this study to recognize that various forms of corruption exist and are very widespread. One of the most common forms involves some kind of bribery. This practice alarms American managers because they tend to view bribery in black and white. In Mexico, the word "bribery" is somewhat ambiguous. For example, if a policeman stops you for a traffic violation, it is often considered more practical to pay a bribe than get a ticket because it frequently takes hours of standing in line at the Department of Transport offices to pay the ticket. Since the amount of the ticket, even with the bribe, is small, people consider it worth paying to save time lost at work or in other pursuits. However, even with the problems involved in paying tickets, more and more Mexicans are accepting the difficulties involved in order to express their disapproval of bribery.

There exists in Mexico a wide range of small payments which fit into the gray zones between tips and bribes. However, blatant requests for large bribes are still made, though they are becoming more and more difficult to get.

Businesses are increasingly wary of transactions where bribes are expected. The problem lies in identifying situations where a small amount may serve as a great motivation to getting a job done. It must be remembered that salaries are very low and good service is greatly appreciated—a small amount is not easily distinguishable from a tip as are some other kinds of bribes.

The extent to which corruption affects the running of a business operation depends on the circumstances and on the executive's skill in diplomacy and persuasion. The executive group generally lays great stress on adherence to a strict code of business ethics for both management and workers. The managers deplore the existence of corruption and dishonesty, which they consider a brake on the progress of their country; but they are aware that its eradication would require a change of basic outlook by a large section of the population, a slow process if possible at all. Within an organization constant vigilance is necessary in order to avoid corrupt and dishonest practices. In addition, reliance is placed on family and *compadrazgo* relationships[1] as a means of assuring trustworthiness and loyalty. However, there are occasions when it is impossible to avoid

---

[1] A *compadre* is someone who is a godfather to one of your children or whose child is your godchild. *Compadrazgo* is the tie thus formed.

dealing with corrupt individuals who may block a perfectly legitimate business operation unless they are in some way rewarded for their cooperation. Such cases are dealt with by Mexican management according to well-established practices. One of the most common involves the compadrazgo relationship in which an executive calls an influential friend who, in turn, uses his influence to solve the problem.

When it comes to telling the truth, the average Mexican's concept is not as absolute as the typical American's. Any given statement may appear completely ethical to a Mexican, whereas to an American it would appear to be a lie. It must be remembered, however, that because of their high degree of interpersonal sensitivity, the first concern of Mexicans is to avoid hurt feelings and confrontation. Therefore, one cannot always get a direct or a completely honest answer to a direct question. In general Mexicans feel that, in the long run, diplomacy and an indirect, discreet response lead to better understanding and achieve more than do blunt truth and direct confrontation.

United States

Traditionally, Americans have been brought up in an atmosphere influenced by the Puritan ethic, which instilled in them a belief that honesty was a principal virtue and that one should tell the truth even when it is unpleasant. If they were caught cheating on tests, students would fail and suffer a reprimand or be expelled.

Teachers were expected to set an example of honesty, fairness, and reliability. Tests were rigorously supervised and graded and transgressions punished. By the time the students left college they had an ingrained sense of the code of ethics demanded by the society.

During the last few decades, significant changes have occurred in the attitudes of Americans toward honesty in school. Cheating is more widespread and more acceptable to students. Major scandals at the military academies have underlined this evolving ethical orientation. It is probably accurate to say that, in general, most Americans disapprove of cheating in school but that it now occurs more often and is acceptable to more people than in past eras.

It is difficult to estimate the import of this change when young people enter the work world. They are exposed to new pressures to compromise their principles because of competition and the drive to acquire wealth and possessions. Although there are cases of padded expense accounts, offers of trips, or memberships in exclusive clubs in exchange for favors, such forms of corruption are not the norm. In the higher echelons, unethical practices are even rarer, but when they are uncovered they raise a public outcry. The average American expects laws to be respected and crime to be punished.

Management Styles

WORK/LEISURE

Mexico

Most Mexicans consider work a necessary evil, necessary in order to earn enough money to satisfy one's needs and those of one's family and, if possible, to leave enough over to enjoy the really important things in life: the pleasures of conviviality with family and friends. Work is, however, an exercise which fills all or most of the daylight hours, so ways have to be found to make it agreeable—which is done by creating a convivial atmosphere in the workplace. The hiring of relatives and friends furthers this aim (and contributes to a mutual sense of reliability and trustworthiness), as do other patterns of Mexican social behavior. Nevertheless, with the growth of larger and more complex enterprises and the consequent pressures for increased efficiency and productivity, the convivial atmosphere has suffered.

These forces have affected the attitudes and responsibilities of executives as well. However, Mexican executives in general still retain their traditional taste for the lighter side of life, both at work and at home. They are convinced that a happy and healthy life requires a balance between work and pleasure, even at the cost of leaving some work for mañana. They therefore try as much as possible to incorporate a certain amount of pure pleasure into their workday.

Because of economic pressures for survival, employees have generally become more work-oriented. This does not mean, however, that they give up what they consider their basic right to enjoy life—even at the expense of their work performance. But they are increasingly conscientious about work and very much concerned about keeping their jobs. For executives, the amount they earn, though important, does not play as strong a role in determining job satisfaction as it does in the United States; status and a congenial working environment are of equal importance. Nevertheless, mobility between companies is motivated predominantly by salary considerations and opportunities for career advancement, since increased income means more possibilities of sharing the good things in life with family and friends.

United States

In general, it is fair to say that U.S. executives live to work, while Mexicans work to live. In the United States work is seen as intrinsically worthwhile and enjoyable, and leisure is considered a reward for work completed. Little time, therefore, is set aside for recreation in the daily life of most U.S. executives.

Since dedication to work is expected to bring financial rewards (which as noted above are related to status), money sometimes becomes an end in itself instead of a means to an end. Many businesspeople dedicate so much of their life to work or work-related activities that they lose their taste for relaxation and recreation and, perhaps worse, sacrifice their family life.

Americans generally prefer not to mix business with pleasure, unless the pleasure involves other business executives and can be considered useful to the business—a business breakfast or lunch, for instance, or a game of golf. Golf is one of the most popular leisure activities of the U.S. executive, and colleagues and business associates often strike business deals while playing. But in general terms, U.S. executives regard work and pleasure as belonging to two different worlds, one involving their tough business image and the other their private, altogether different personal image.

DIRECTION/SUPERVISION

Mexico

Mexican executives have great respect for authority. Their upbringing has inculcated in them an acceptance of absolute authority on the part of parents and, at times, elders. As a result, young executives never question or even comment on a decision of their superiors, even if they totally disagree with it. Nor do superiors normally accept such questioning from subordinates. Typical comments by Mexican executives are: "Subordinates are expected to accept unconditionally what their bosses say, even though they might disagree"; or "If the boss says the paper is green, then it is green"; or simply, "The Mexican does as he is told."

In Mexico there is no tradition of delegation of authority; the concept itself is alien to most people. The boss is an extension of the autocratic, authoritarian father image. As a result, delegation of responsibility normally takes the form of assignment of specific tasks, which are carried out in constant consultation with one's superior. Most subordinates prefer this approach, since it saves them from making errors and from losing face. This is summed up by a comment from a Mexican executive: "Subordinates feel insecure and are afraid of making mistakes."

The smaller firms are nearly all completely autocratic. The larger companies, on the other hand, have become so complex that the delegation of responsibility for an area, and even some actual authority, have become a necessity. Nevertheless, even in the largest companies, authority is, for the most part, still vested in a very few at the top. One finds considerable delegation of responsibility but rarely the authority to go with it.

It must, nevertheless, be pointed out that a new generation of managers is growing up in Mexico which, because of university training and modern attitudes, strongly supports the practice of delegation of responsibility together with the accompanying authority, backed up by the necessary accountability. Where this more participative approach has been introduced, it has generally met with success. The shift is slow in taking place, but it is widely felt to be essential for business effectiveness in an increasingly competitive economy.

United States

In the United States, people are brought up to be independent and enjoy making their own decisions. Young executives are thus generally reluctant to ask for advice and want to be given as much responsibility and authority as possible. They dislike authority being exercised over them and do not like having to obtain approval for their every action. They feel competent and want to be permitted to make most decisions themselves. They find great stimulation in tackling new problems alone, and they thrive on the challenge of situations where decisions are tested. They feel secure in their knowledge and know that a minor error will not lose them the support and respect of their superiors, because making a few mistakes in the beginning is considered normal in the learning process.

THEORY VERSUS PRACTICE

Mexico

As mentioned earlier, Mexicans are by nature theorists, that is, they enjoy the intellectual pursuit of abstract concepts. They have an extremely well-developed ability to conceptualize and perceive problems in global terms, identifying all the influences and visualizing their ramifications. When a new project is launched, it is presented with great pride and is usually the occasion for a festive gathering of executives, subordinates, and others. But the practicalities of implementation and problem solving in everyday business situations are generally not addressed. Most senior executives know in general terms what is needed, but many have difficulty in passing on their knowledge to their subordinates in a detailed, organized fashion. Problems arise because managers are expected to implement plans which they do not fully understand, and they also often lack the management tools to carry them out. The consequences manifest themselves in a number of different ways.

1. Programs and projects, conceived, planned and produced on paper, are often not put into practice or are left uncompleted because of unforeseen difficulties.

2. Problems are left unsolved, resulting in lower productivity and a negative effect on personal motivation.
3. Workers become apathetic because they rarely see the projects, announced with such fanfare, become a reality.
4. Supervisors lose credibility because in the eyes of their workers they do not keep their promises.
5. Middle management becomes frustrated because it lacks the authority and the necessary tools to implement the approved program.
6. Senior executives are dissatisfied because they feel they have done their planning job, but subordinates have been incapable of implementing the project.

Interestingly, most senior executives are unaware of their difficulties in translating plans into concrete action. They usually perceive their difficulties as the inability of the subordinates to understand their instructions correctly. They feel that the subordinates are the ones at fault if things do not happen the way they should. Rarely would they associate the difficulty with their own inadequacy as developers of people.

Most of the larger companies are now laying great stress on bridging this theory/practice gap. Improvement is already apparent, especially in companies which have entered the export market. But it remains a continuing challenge, particularly in view of the lack of practical orientation in schools and universities and their failure to teach the analytical skills needed for problem solving. Attempts are now being made to bring about closer collaboration between the business community and the universities in order to improve teaching and promote an understanding of the needs of the business world. Up to the present, however, collaboration has been limited mainly to technical fields.

United States

Throughout their education and training, U.S. executives have been exposed to an analytical approach to problem solving and to an emphasis on practical applications, and this background serves them well in the business world. At the university level they are introduced to complex theoretical or conceptual issues, often in the form of analyzing somewhat idealized business situations, but, even here, practical applications of the theory are emphasized.

Once graduates enter the business world, the adjustment required of them is far less than for their Latin counterparts. In their daily business affairs, they are confronted with a fast-moving, action-oriented world where there is little time to spend on theorizing about the problems encountered. The pressures are too great. Their approach, instead, is largely empirical; what action needs to be taken is based on an examination of the facts of the situation. The majority of executives are primarily involved in the setting and achieving of action-oriented objectives. Only the most senior executives are concerned with long-range planning and broad strategy issues and, even there, little use is made of theory.

CONTROL

Mexico

The whole concept of control and follow-through is comparatively new in Mexico. As a carryover from the traditional attitude of craftsmen, workers are unaccustomed to checking on their work. Quality is assured by the craftsman's skill and in most cases does not have to meet rigid standards. Delivery schedules are elastic enough to accommodate avoidable as well as unavoidable delays. However, with the increased sophistication of industry, the complexity of the products it supplies, and the pressures of more intense competition, this situation is rapidly changing. Consistent procedures for quality control and follow-through have become a necessity. Cultural considerations, however, often require adaptations before they can be effectively incorporated into Mexican business operations.

One part of the problem stems from the interpersonal sensitivity of most Mexican executives. Subordinates are inclined to feel that their superiors do not trust them if procedures are introduced which are designed to check on the subordinate's performance. A typical reaction is "Why should my boss check on me? Doesn't he trust me?" Bosses, on the other hand, often feel it beneath their dignity to keep checking on tasks which have already been delegated and are the responsibility of the subordinate. It is only when something goes wrong that remedial action is taken, and then the blame is shifted as far down the ladder as possible. This style and its attendant problems permeate many organizations, from top management through the middle echelons and supervisors right down to the shop-floor foremen. Even where follow-through procedures exist, they are not always implemented. Top management is generally aware of the importance of control and follow-through, but the training of staff in the appropriate procedures is proving to be a slow and difficult task because of the cultural reconditioning involved. Thus, many industrial firms continue to be plagued by inconsistent product quality and uncertain delivery times. In the tough competition for export markets, these problems are major liabilities, and an increasing number of Mexican companies are making all-out efforts to overcome them, often with great success.

United States

The highly sophisticated control and follow-through systems used by all major U.S. business organizations—not just the manufacturing sector—are a key factor in assuring their efficiency and competitiveness. Every efficient company regards an effective system of checks and controls as indispensable to its survival.

The market demands consistent quality and reliable delivery schedules. For profitability it is essential that inventory be kept to a minimum and that work flow smoothly. These requirements can only be met through tight controls and follow-through procedures. Employees become so steeped in the concept of control that it becomes almost automatic. Checking is done at every stage of the production process so that errors are detected close to their source, before additional operations have added to the cost. Rapid evaluation and reporting procedures ensure constant feedback of results to management in a manner which interferes as little as possible with production. Pressures are considerable, since defective products or reduced productivity are immediately reflected in reduced output and the consequent loss of competitive edge.

STAFFING ──────────────────────────

Mexico

Employment in Mexico is concentrated in the private sector, 80 percent of which consists of small or medium-sized, family-run companies. (Since GATT and NAFTA there has been a dramatic reduction in the number of government-owned businesses.) But in all Mexican businesses, from the largest to the smallest, hiring practices strongly favor relatives and friends of employees and avoid, as far as possible, unknown or unrecommended persons. Inevitably, though, as companies have grown in size, they have found it necessary to hire staff from "outside." The use of newspaper want ads is now quite common. Nevertheless, few higher-level executive positions are filled without some personal knowledge of the candidate, even though a few executive placement agencies now operate. But it is to be remembered that trustworthiness, loyalty, and reliability are of paramount importance to employers, causing them to continue to rely on family and compadrazgo ties.

United States

Recruitment of personnel is generally done by open competition. This policy, employers feel, ensures the selection of the best available candidate from the widest possible labor market. In general the U.S. executive feels strongly that an efficient organization requires separation of the work life of its employees from their personal lives. Hiring relatives and friends of employees is generally frowned upon, and in most large companies it is carefully restricted. Many years of experience have convinced U.S. executives of the inadvisability of hiring relatives and friends. Some of the reasons: (a) charges of nepotism or favoritism may arise, causing resentment among other employees, (b) involvement of the friends or relatives in conflicts between employee and employer, and (c) danger of collusion.

LOYALTY

Mexico

Historically, the loyalty of Mexican workers has been based on devotion to the *patron,* or boss—the owner of the business. On that person rested the welfare of the worker and his family, be it for food, clothing, or medical needs. The boss was even consulted on personal problems. Not all bosses were paternalistic; indeed, there were many cases of shameful exploitation. However, as a result of the Mexican Revolution and the birth of social security,[2] accompanied by an accelerated growth of business and industry, this comprehensive "welfare" system has all but disappeared; consequently, the worker's loyalty to boss and company is eroding. Survival now depends on one's own efforts—the trend toward what in Mexico is called "self-loyalty."

At the executive level there is more evidence of loyalty to the organization, because the executive's position and salary are closely linked with the fortunes of the business. Nevertheless, these loyalties are not unconditional, as witnessed by the increasing mobility of high executives between organizations (but less between geographical areas). Such moves are mostly in response to an opportunity for a position of greater responsibility and salary, but a considerable number are also caused by dissatisfaction with company policies or practices, or by interpersonal conflicts.

In the average organization, a worker's loyalty depends largely on the personnel policies, including pay, and the extent to which the organization succeeds in establishing a friendly working atmosphere. All the evidence available to this author indicates clearly that organizations with good human relations policies and practices experience considerable employee loyalty and low turnover. Those where human relations are given a low priority command little loyalty and experience a consid-

---

[2]Mexican social security provides medical and hospital services, pensions, and limited unemployment coverage for state and private employees and their families. For the millions of people outside the formal economy, there is no social security or welfare.

erably higher turnover. Nearly all the executives interviewed emphasized the importance of capable, human relations-oriented management in maintaining a loyal and motivated work force.

United States

Because of their individualistic nature and the need to show personal achievement as a basis for advancement, U.S. executives are first and foremost loyal to themselves. They will work extremely hard in a business firm and perform outstandingly; however, the effort is generally not expended for the sake of the firm, but principally to improve their chances of advancement. If they cannot progress rapidly enough within a particular organization, they will seek advancement by moving to another. This practice leads to significant executive mobility, with every move intended to bring more responsibility and higher earnings. U.S. executives do, of course, sometimes move for other reasons, such as dissatisfaction with a company's way of doing things or preference for a different geographical location. But executives cannot move too often, or they will be labeled unstable.

COMPETITION

Mexico

Mexican executives are not strongly competitive in the sense of wanting to surpass the performance of their colleagues. They value more a friendly, relaxed atmosphere at work, free of conflict and confrontation (which they try to avoid whenever possible). The unpleasantness which would result from stepping on a colleague's toes to gain recognition for superior achievement is distasteful to them. In any case, the road to promotion in most organizations is still more by way of influence than by outstanding achievement. Since merit alone is usually not sufficient, competition frequently takes another form, i.e., political maneuvering and ingratiating oneself with the right people.

United States

U.S. executives typically thrive on the stimulus of competition. They are, for the most part, extremely ambitious, which often results in what Mexicans may see as a lack of consideration for other people. They feel pressured by the highly competitive environment in which they live, and to "get there first" sometimes requires stepping on someone else's toes. This competitiveness naturally varies from profession to profession, but it is extremely high in the field of business. The resulting tensions frequently affect the interpersonal relationships of business executives and are also reflected in the high incidence of stress-related illnesses.

Nevertheless, most younger executives enjoy a competitive environment and feel that it does, for the most part, make for high-quality performance, a healthy business, and a strong economy.

TRAINING AND DEVELOPMENT

Mexico

Executive development is a recent concept in Mexico. In the traditional family-owned firm, the son learned from the father, and knowledge was acquired gradually, through experience (or perhaps by osmosis), until the father retired and the son took over. Relatives and friends completed the management team. However, as business organizations began to grow and become more complex, the need arose for an increasing number of competent executives. Candidates for executive positions had to be found from outside the family circle, marking the beginnings of executive development within a firm. The responsibility for the passing on of knowledge and skills was assumed by the older and more experienced employees.

In recent years educational institutions have started offering courses in management, which has raised the academic standard of new entrants into management positions. Unfortunately, there is wide variation in the quality of the education provided, and usually the theoretical concepts learned are not accompanied by training in how to translate them into practical applications. This means that the business community still has to shoulder a great part of the training responsibility.

Unfortunately, apart from a few large companies, there are no structured training programs for the development of these young graduates. They are usually hired for specific vacancies and, if they prove themselves, they may be considered for promotion. In the process of proving themselves they must perform their assigned duties to their superiors' complete satisfaction; but above all they have to show unquestioning devotion to their superiors, who must judge them as trustworthy, pleasant, and cooperative. Promotion depends mainly on this relationship; and once promoted, the young executives must again do everything to please their new superiors and continue to do so over many years.

For those who are members of the employer's family, on the other hand, this process is much accelerated. Shorter periods of time are spent in different areas of the company, and movement to a senior executive position is quick. In general, young executives know that promotion depends more on influence and politics than on achievement. They therefore endeavor to please the boss and whoever else may have influence on their getting ahead. As a result, executive positions are not necessarily filled by those whose records show outstanding performance but by those most adept at the political maneuvering mentioned above.

However, most of the larger companies are now attaching more importance to professional qualifications and proven achievement as a basis for hiring and promotion. They are also placing greater stress on executive training and development. Many executives have been exposed to some management training, especially in staff supervision. Usually provided by trainers from outside the company, these programs most often take the form of a lecture, followed by a discussion and the distribution of notes covering the basic points of the lecture. Case studies are gradually being introduced, though few good Mexican-oriented case studies exist. Most participants in these courses are eager to learn and are pleased they have been selected for training. They also value the impressive certificate which normally marks the completion of a course.

The main problem with this training is that the subject matter is almost invariably treated from a general and theoretical, rather than a practical, point of view, so that the trainee seldom gets concrete ideas on how to deal with specific problems. The benefits most participants derive, therefore, are limited. The ability to offer effective training is also restricted by the great disparities in age and educational background to be found among the managers being trained. Supervisors who have been with the company thirty years or more, for instance, may have had only eight years or so of schooling. "The supervisory group," said one executive, echoing a widely held opinion, "is the most difficult to train, and the one that needs it most."

In general, Mexican executives have not been accustomed to viewing the training of subordinates as an integral part of their responsibilities. In recent years the importance of training has been recognized, but for most Mexican executives the word "training" means formal instruction in which participants are taken away from the workplace and exposed to an outside expert who will give them the solutions to their problems. The lack of confidence managers display relative to taking charge of the training of their subordinates stems not simply from the feeling that they don't have the knowledge needed (which they, in fact, often do have), but rather from a deep-seated feeling that training requires an especially qualified teacher. Any training that does take place in the business setting usually occurs at departmental meetings, where pertinent problems are discussed.

United States

For many years U.S. business organizations have recruited their future executives from the universities, so that the executive group is now almost wholly composed of college graduates, many with postgraduate degrees or some work at the postgraduate level. Many students major in business administration, and even those who don't often take management courses. In any event, they all come from an educational system highly oriented toward the practical application of the education and training they have received. In addition, the educational and social setting in the United States is such that most people see further education and personal and professional development beyond college as desirable.

Young prospective executives are therefore ready for the management development programs available at most large U.S. companies. Under these programs, training and evaluation procedures are set up, beginning with the arrival of new management trainees and continuing through their first two or three years of work. During this time they are given specific assignments at a responsible level in different areas of the firm, and their work performance is periodically submitted to strict evaluation. Following this initial training period, they are usually offered junior management positions, but training and/or outside course work continue if they are considered useful in rounding out the young managers' educational background.

U.S. executives accept the training of their own staff as an important responsibility, and the training function of an executive rates high in the evaluation of a good manager. However, not all managers carry it out efficiently, because they do not give it a high enough priority. Training effectiveness is increasingly measured in quantitative terms related to productivity. This measurement is considered important because of the requirement that the results justify the cost of the training.

The occupational mobility that characterizes the U.S. business milieu raises a dilemma relative to the strong emphasis on training. Executives trained in one firm may be attracted to a more senior or better-paid position in another. The investment in time and money by the initial employers will be lost if the executives move. But generally, the larger organizations accept the loss of a percentage of the people they have trained, and they will, in turn, attract people trained by other companies. The resulting cross-fertilization of ideas is seen as beneficial by management.

TIME

Mexico

Traditionally, time is an imprecise concept in Mexico. The attitude toward it is perhaps best summed up in the word "mañana," meaning not today, but not necessarily tomorrow either. There is little awareness of the pressure of time or any sense of urgency in getting things done. Also, there is little objective importance attached to time commitments. For example, you may be told "Your shoes will be ready tomorrow." The shoemaker wants to make you happy by saying this, but realistically he knows that it is not very likely because he is too busy or has more important things to do first.

A firm may say "Yes, your shipment will be ready on Tuesday." You arrive on Tuesday to pick it up but find it is not ready. No one is upset or embarrassed; they politely explain that the paperwork has not yet been processed, or they give some similar explanation.

Time commitments are considered desirable objectives but not binding promises. Little concern is felt for the time wasted by the client in waiting or for the inconvenience of making several trips to accomplish a single task. There is always another day.[3]

Yet this attitude toward time is beginning to change among modern Mexican professionals. As lifestyles become more complex and pressures for greater productivity increase, people are beginning to feel more concern for punctuality, and time commitments are more frequently met. But this is a slow process, and the general feeling still is "What we don't get done today will keep until tomorrow."

The disregard for time reaches its pinnacle in government departments and public sector enterprises, where most procedures require long forms to be filled out, long letters to be filed, and endless waits in line. The effect this has on business deserves a study by itself.

---

[3]Socially, time and courtesy are closely related. For example, it would be considered bad manners to arrive at someone's home punctually at the hour indicated. A half hour after is about right, though one can also come later. Invitations only indicate arrival time, never departure time, as it would be considered impolite to tell the guests when to leave. Unless guests feel they can stay as long as they like, they do not feel welcome.

United States

Since "time is money" and since money is what business is all about, every decision, every activity, every commitment—whether at work or at home—is controlled by the clock. The executive is under constant pressure to meet time commitments, and much of his or her personal life is thereby sacrificed. Lack of punctuality is considered almost a disgrace, and excuses are seldom accepted. Verbal commitments are considered as binding as written ones. Life moves by the clock, and any disrespect for time has severe repercussions. Everyday work life is often referred to as a treadmill: to succeed you must stay on it; if you step off, you are lost.[4]

It is well-known that this concept of time dominates the lives of the U.S. business community. The consequent need to treat time as a precious resource has given birth to the discipline of time management, which has been the subject of many books. Most Mexican executives are very conscious of this concept when dealing with their U.S. counterparts.

PLANNING

Mexico

Planning has always been difficult in Mexico because of the extreme fluctuations in the economic and political climate, ranging from spectacular booms to deep depressions. Many companies have benefited in the periods of expansion, not because of any long-term planning, but because their management has known how to take advantage of the circumstances by making short-term pragmatic decisions and by taking considerable risks. But for every company that has prospered, there are sev-

---

[4]When it comes to social commitments, the American's concept of time is much more precise than the Mexican's. Most visits are made with the understanding that guests will arrive at or soon after the hour stipulated. To arrive very late is considered impolite. It is also quite common to indicate the time the guests are expected to leave if the event is an open house or cocktail party. Unless specifically asked by the hosts, it is impolite to stay longer.

eral that have suffered financially or gone under. Still, today, in small and even medium-sized companies, almost all planning is short-range. The average Mexican executive is accustomed to dealing with crisis situations.

Even with the passage of NAFTA, very little has changed in the way in which the average Mexican company is regulated by the government. Small and medium-sized companies, especially, are heavily burdened by government-imposed administrative red tape which changes frequently. There are also very heavy tax burdens. This situation puts them at a disadvantage when trying to compete with their U.S. counterparts. In addition, these companies have become seriously decapitalized through years of economic uncertainty and, especially at present, the high cost of credit. As a result, companies cannot afford to borrow to improve and modernize their operations as they must if they are to survive. A considerable number of small businesses went bankrupt following Mexico's entry into GATT in 1986. It is estimated now that many, if not the majority, will not be able to survive the competition from foreign goods and services entering Mexico under NAFTA. On the other hand, larger businesses are in a better situation, and most have been able to negotiate more favorable terms. This sector is also the one which is mainly involved in the export market as well as being able to compete successfully with foreign businesses within the country. Most of these have anticipated the changes coming and have modernized their operations in order to compete.

Large numbers of people in the working population who have lost their jobs in small businesses have gravitated to the "informal" sector, which stands at over 30 percent of production. Others have migrated to the large cities or the U.S. border region in search of work.

NAFTA has placed the survival of the small-business sector in Mexico at considerable risk. Based on recent analyses of the situation, it is considered probable that a large proportion of this sector will disappear. From a cultural standpoint, this is a great concern because the social stability of the country and the major source of employment depend on the health of the small-business sector. Even the ones which have modernized do not have much hope of competing with larger foreign companies offering similar products or services. In addition to the small-business sector, the poor farmers, peasants, laborers, and the unemployed have nothing and are rarely able to think beyond daily survival. This sector consists of a cross-section of people living in both the cities and the countryside, and at present stands at about 50 percent of the population. Fortunately, attention is beginning to be given to these people. The poor thus represent an important factor in the long-term political, cultural, and social stability of Mexico.

United States

Comparatively speaking, in U.S. companies long-term planning, in which overseas operations are included, is considered basic to the success of any business, though this does not exclude making tactical adjustments as the need arises. This practice has been made possible by the relatively stable U.S. economic and political climate. Interestingly, even U.S. businesses have recently been criticized—in comparison with the Japanese, for instance—for not planning far enough ahead.

It should be noted, however, that when U.S. executives are transferred abroad, usually on a two- to three-year assignment, they have to shift their thinking. They know their standing within the corporate structure will depend on the results achieved during their tenure. They are thus under pressure to plan the short term and to show improvement in the financial performance of the operation, even if it may be to the detriment of the long-term interests of the organization.

Major Issues in Cross-Cultural Management

Conducting a business operation in Mexico requires great flexibility on both the U.S. and Mexican sides. Both must be ready to change and adapt. The U.S. executive will find that the greatest adjustments he or she will have to make concern the most deeply rooted cultural aspects of Mexican society. Many of these do not conflict with modern management practices, but others do to a greater or lesser degree. In those areas where there is a conflict, appropriate adaptation is necessary on both sides to maintain a well-motivated, productive work force. On the Mexican side, the major effort of adaptation lies in the assimilation of the basic techniques and attitudes of modern management.

A few Mexican and U.S. executives have already made the necessary adjustments and are reaping the benefits in increased efficiency and productivity, but the majority are still searching for the key to the misunderstandings, conflicts, and inefficiencies which plague their joint endeavors.

What follows is a summary of the major cultural and management issues which create the gap between Americans and Mexicans in the work environment. If the gap is to be bridged, these issues must be understood and dealt with. Some practical suggestions for doing so appear both in this discussion and in appendix A.

CULTURAL ISSUES —————————————————————————

Family

Considering the central role the family plays in Mexican life, it is unlikely that any significant change will take place in this area. For Mexicans, family relationships come before everything else, and foreign executives who expect to be successful must accept that priority and take their employees' family concerns seriously. They need to listen carefully and express interest and concern about their subordinates' families; they should expect occasional absences when there is illness in the family. In general, they should be alert to the possibility of finding in family ties and concerns an explanation for behavior they don't understand.

Education

The Mexican educational system is attempting to introduce a more analytical approach, at least in the sciences, but there is little evidence that much change is occurring. Under the circumstances, Mexican university graduates take up their jobs in business with a radically different outlook from that of their U.S. counterparts—and they will continue to do so for a long time.

Foreign executives, therefore, simply have to accept the fact that if they are going to get their Mexican managers to think more analytically and adopt a problem-solving approach, they will have to provide the training themselves. In their executive-development programs, specific provisions for this transition should be included. This topic is discussed further in the section on management training and development.

Personal Sensitivity

The personal sensitivity of Mexicans is well-known and has frequently been identified as a source of difficulty in relations between Mexico and the United States. Tact and diplomacy are called for on the part of Americans if they are to avoid alienating their Mexican subordinates. In particular, they need to resist saying outright, "You are wrong." Mexicans know perfectly well when they have made a mistake, but verbalizing it puts them to shame and is liable to make them withdraw. On the other hand, it is important for U.S. executives to admit when they are wrong because this will go a long way in demonstrating to the Mexican that they are also human. In addition, it is important to find reasons to praise Mexican subordinates in order to balance the many situations where criticism is expressed. Experience has shown that praise, in Mexico, even for small things, is highly motivating.

Aesthetics

The basic aesthetic nature of Mexican executives is not likely to change, nor is their preference for abstractions over that which is concrete. Both aspects are, however, being gradually modified as a result of work pressures. This transition can be speeded up through well-conceived training programs under the guidance of sensitive, human relations-oriented U.S. managers (who are, unfortunately, rare). On the other hand, foreign executives must not lose sight of the potential benefits when the Mexican manager's creativity is channeled productively. The ideas put forth by the Mexicans should always be examined carefully to see if they can be usefully put into practice.

Ethics

In Mexican culture, as in many other cultures around the world, saving face is important. Every response is conditioned by the need to avoid hurt feelings—one's own and other people's. This frequently leads to evasive replies, half answers, and "white lies." To a U.S. executive, brought up to value openness, directness, and, above all, honesty in business dealings, this can be very disconcerting and often causes problems. It is important for Mexicans to realize that they do not lose face in the eyes of a U.S. boss if they admit a mistake, but that they are more likely to lose that respect by evading the question and being found out later. An American needs to understand the degree to which Mexicans will resist opening up to people with whom they are not personally close. Tact is of major importance in efforts to get at the truth, as is the establishment of a relationship of mutual trust. Most managers find that once a relationship of confidence exists, their Mexican colleagues become more open and direct in their responses. In the words of one U.S. manager, "Once the Mexican trusts you and has complete confidence in you as a person, he will be your most valued confidant." This topic is discussed further in the individual versus task issue which follows.

MANAGEMENT ISSUES ——————————————————

Individual versus Task

Mexican executives are essentially person-oriented. They base their judgment of their U.S. superiors first and foremost on their personal qualities. The Mexican must feel that his boss is *buena gente* (roughly translated as a "nice guy"—see "Mr. Wygard's Story" on page xi)—before he gives him his wholehearted support. U.S. executives, on the other hand, are basically task-oriented. They value their business associates primarily for their performance, often viewing them as tools to carry out tasks or to accomplish certain objectives.

U.S. executives will have to take the first step by demonstrating a genuine personal interest in their Mexican colleagues in order to earn their respect and confidence. Once that happens, the Mexican executives will in most cases become dedicated and hardworking collaborators. Most U.S. managers in Mexico agree that, particularly at the beginning, it is extremely important to listen attentively to and ask questions of their Mexican associates, not only concerning work, but also about their families (see page 62), customs, and traditions. It is important to remember that for Mexicans social conventions come first and work, second!

Theory versus Practice

This is one of the most important areas of adjustment for Mexican managers. It is essential for them to make the difficult transition from abstract theorizing to a more practical approach. U.S. executives can help them by implementing carefully conceived management development programs and by offering their Mexican subordinates continuous personal encouragement. This can be a time-consuming process because it means working closely with the Mexicans, reviewing their progress, and encouraging them at each step. It usually requires taking one topic at a time, treating it in depth, and clearly demonstrating its applicability in real situations.

Feedback

Mexican managers are accustomed to giving only positive feedback to their superiors and to expressing only views which coincide with theirs. Mexican executives would consider it disrespectful of a subordinate to contradict them. U.S. executives, on the other hand, expect subordinates to tell them the bad news as well as the good. They want to be informed of problems as soon as they occur in order to take timely remedial action. Most are receptive to reasoned disagreement. Any ideas which might improve the operation are welcomed, and they are considered on their merits.

Mexican executives, once they overcome the feeling that they are showing disrespect if they don't confirm their superiors' opinions, enjoy participating in the decision-making process, but it must take place in an atmosphere of mutual confidence and respect.

Appointments and Promotions

As should be quite clear to the reader by now, trust and close personal relationships (especially family ties) are critical to the success of most undertakings in Mexico. "You must remember," one Mexican executive said, "that it is difficult to find anybody you can trust outside the family and close friends." This statement sounds strange to Americans, who base a steady stream of business decisions on trust in people they know only superficially. Yet, in Mexico, this dependence on family and close friends is real. Nevertheless, things are changing in Mexico. There is increasing pressure on companies to operate efficiently and with maximum productivity so that performance standards are becoming as high for friends and family as for anyone else. U.S. managers do not have great difficulty in dealing with friends and relatives of employees when they make it clear to their Mexican employees that promotions are made on the basis of performance.

Delegation and Supervision

Mexican owners and senior managers assign areas of work or specific tasks to subordinates who do what they have been told and do not have (nor are they allowed) to think for themselves. Because of this practice, senior managers delegate responsibility for a job but retain authority for decision making. Subordinates therefore cannot be held accountable in the true sense of the word. They feel accountable for carrying out the specific instructions, but not the consequences. This way of managing is very different from the U.S. style. The whole area of effective delegation and supervision techniques thus requires considerable development in Mexico. The junior executive needs the knowledge and the self-confidence to take on heavy responsibilities, while the U.S. manager has to develop the rapport necessary for guiding the transition. This is not a rapid process. It must be understood that the subordinate wants to please his boss and thus prefers to stop and ask for advice rather than make a mistake. Therefore, it is important that explanations are unambiguous and fully understood. On the other hand, the young executive should be brought into the decision-making process as early as possible and be convinced that accepting responsibilities is to his benefit.

Control and Follow-Through

Once rapport has been established between the U.S. and Mexican executives, the Mexicans will generally become drawn in to the planning and implementation processes. After that the establishment of control and follow-through procedures becomes less of a problem, because the Mexican managers can see that it makes their job easier and their workers more productive. As subordinates become more interested in their own work, they become more concerned with quality and start checking their work more conscientiously. The few Mexican companies that have so far made this transition have achieved levels of quality and productivity equaling or even surpassing those of similar U.S. plants. Their example demonstrates the enormous potential of the Mexican work force. In fostering this transition, the key is the U.S. manager's daily involvement in the development and training of his Mexican managerial group.

This will overcome the resistance to "checking" and "being checked" and build the trust which will in turn help Mexican executives get over their fear of losing face if they admit to an error. As Mexican executives accept greater responsibility along with the concomitant authority and accountability, they will naturally exercise control and will follow through on their own initiative.

Word versus Deed

Mexican executives still tend to feel that a well-intentioned word is an acceptable substitute for action. They often lack a strong sense of commitment to what they say they intend to do. They usually consider their word a desirable goal but feel no disgrace if problems delay or prevent its realization in practice. This contrasts with the attitude of Americans, who are interested primarily in deeds. They consider their word a binding commitment to action.

In this area Mexican executives have to learn to be more realistic and less optimistic. They have to be cautioned to base their commitments on conservative estimates, allowing for unforeseen problems, and then be held accountable for the action taken. They are so used to saying what they think will make their superior happy that they sometimes forget what can be realistically accomplished. Initially, U.S. managers need to follow up on all actions so as to make sure word is followed by deed.

Time

In a modern business enterprise, strict adherence to time schedules is imperative, and Mexican managers and the work force must be convinced of this. Patience is called for on the part of U.S. executives while Mexican attitudes toward time change, and plans must take into account time slippages. Time estimates must not only be realistic but should include a cushion for the unanticipated.

Management Training and Development

Effective management training is one of the crucial issues in any Mexican business operation. It is also one of the most difficult aspects of management responsibility for the U.S. expatriate executive. Because of their different backgrounds, training, and business exposure, the Mexican executive brings to his job a set of attitudes entirely different from those of his U.S. counterpart. These subconscious attitudes can, and often do, block the assimilation of modern management techniques. It is therefore desirable to start off the training process with some form of self-analysis which brings these attitudes into the open.

The next step is to scrutinize the training program and material for cultural bias and carefully adapt them to the environment in which they are to be used. This is especially true of any case studies used as training aids. Most available case studies are culturally oriented to the United States and make little sense in a Mexican setting.

In addition, the transition from theory to practice will be made more smoothly and effectively if the training is performed in short sessions, interspersed with periods of direct practical application. Step-by-step monitoring of the results and recognition given for progress will help in maintaining motivation.

On the whole, Mexican executives are receptive and eager to learn new techniques and appreciate being given the opportunity for training. However, they can easily be discouraged if they feel they are having American ideas and values forced down their throats without regard for their own culture and traditions.

COMPARATIVE TABLE—CULTURAL FACTORS

Feature	Mexico	U.S.
Family	Family is first priority	Family usually second to work
	Children sheltered	Children independent
	Executive mobility limited	Executive mobility unrestricted
Religion	Long Roman Catholic tradition	Mixed religions
	Fatalistic outlook	"Master of own life" outlook

Feature	*Mexico*	*U.S.*
Education	Memorization	Analytical approach
	Theoretical emphasis	Practical emphasis
	Rigid, broad curriculum	Narrow, in-depth specialization
Nationalism	Very nationalistic	Very patriotic
	Proud of long history and traditions	Proud of "American way of life"
	Reluctant to settle outside Mexico	Assumes everyone shares his/her materialistic values
Emotional sensitivity	Sensitive to differences of opinion	Separates work from emotions
	Fears loss of face	Sensitivity seen as weakness
	Shuns confrontation	Puts up tough business front
Etiquette	Old-world formality	Formality often sacrificed for efficiency
	Etiquette considered measure of breeding	"Let's get to the point" approach
Grooming	Dress and grooming are status symbols	As long as appearance is reasonable, performance is most important
Status	Title and position more important than money in eyes of society	Money is main status indicator and is reward for achievement
Aesthetics	Aesthetic side of life is important even at work	No time for "useless frills"

Feature	Mexico	U.S.
Ethics	Truth tempered by need for diplomacy	Direct yes/no answers given and expected
	Truth is a relative concept	Truth seen as absolute value

COMPARATIVE TABLE—MANAGEMENT STYLE

Feature	Mexico	U.S.
Work/Leisure	Works to live	Lives to work
	Leisure considered essential for full life	Leisure seen as reward for hard work
	Money is for enjoying life	Money often an end in itself
Direction/ Delegation	Traditional managers autocratic	Managers delegate responsibility and authority
	Younger managers starting to delegate responsibility	Executive seeks responsibility and accepts accountability
	Subordinates used to being assigned tasks, not given authority	
Theory versus practice	Basically theoretical mind	Basically pragmatic mind
	Practical implementation often difficult	Action-oriented, problem-solving approach
Control	Still not fully accepted	Universally accepted and practiced
	Sensitive to being "checked upon"	

Feature	*Mexico*	*U.S.*
Competition	Avoids personal competition; favors harmony at work	Enjoys proving her-/himself in competitive situations
Training and development	Training highly theoretical	Training concrete, specific
	Few structured programs	Structured programs widely used
Time	Relative concept	Categorical imperative
	Deadlines flexible	Deadlines and commitments are firm
Staffing	Family and friends favored because of trustworthiness	Relatives usually barred, favoritism not acceptable
	Promotions based on loyalty to superior	Promotion based on performance
Loyalty	Mostly loyal to superior (person rather than organization)	Mainly self-loyalty
	Beginnings of self-loyalty	Performance motivated by ambition
Planning	Mostly short-term	Mostly long-term

COMPARATIVE TABLE—EDUCATIONAL LEVELS

Feature	*Mexico*	*U.S.*
National median	5 years	12 years
Educational structure	Primary - 6 years Junior high - 3 years (*Secundaria*) Senior high - 3 years (*Preparatoria*) University - 4 years	Elementary - 6 years Junior high - 3 years Senior high - 3 years University - 4 years
Teacher education	Primary teachers have high school plus teacher's college University and most senior high teachers have first university degree; a few have higher degrees	All elementary and high school teachers are university graduates All university faculty have higher degrees
Executives	Large companies: most executives are university graduates and a few have postgraduate study Smaller firms: some executives are university graduates, many of older generation have only senior high school degrees	All executives are university graduates and many have postgraduate study

Feature	Mexico	U.S.
Middle management	Great variation in levels	Four-year university, or two-year college degree
	Many junior executives are graduates; nearly all have completed high school plus further studies	
	In supervisory group, younger generation mostly have senior high and/or technical school degrees; older generation often have less education	
Workers	All have completed primary and some, junior high; in Monterrey area educational levels are generally higher than elsewhere	Nearly all have completed senior high school
Office and secretarial	All have at least completed junior high and training in typing; most have shorthand and elementary book-keeping skills	All have senior high, junior college or university degree, and/or other office skills

Part III

Mr. Smith and Sr. González Have Second Thoughts

It is now six months since Mr. Smith and Sr. González unburdened themselves in letters to their friends. Things have changed since that time.

Both men have gained new insight by coming to grips with the problems and issues as they are discussed in the pages of this book. Here are two subsequent fictional letters in which they write about their mutual cross-cultural business experiences.

Another Letter from Mr. Smith

Dear Bob,

Your great news, that you are also being transferred to Mexico, really caught me by surprise. Perhaps we shall even be able to see each other one of these days.

I have learned a great deal during my first year here. Perhaps it would be helpful if I gave you a few tips about what to expect—things I have had to learn the hard way, and it has been painful, believe me! I owe much of what I have learned to my finance manager, Sr. González. Remember, he's the one who speaks very good English and who served as my channel of communication at the outset. After months of hitting my head against a brick wall, I was feeling totally demoralized. At the end of one particularly frustrating day, I happened to stop by Sr. González's office. We ended up going out for a drink, which turned out to be a very good idea. We relaxed and began really talking to each other. I was amazed at what he said (with considerable encouragement on my part). His comments and some soul-searching on my own have led to a lot of insights into how you run a business in Mexico. Since then, things have been improving, in some ways almost incredibly—thank God!

Anyway, one of the first things you want to do (preferably before you get here) is get yourself a good book on Mexican history and culture. It is really important to understand how different the background and traditions of the Mexicans are from ours. Also, start studying Spanish immediately. That may sound like a big order for a busy executive, but it will give you a real advantage in dealing with your staff, even if you don't know much at the outset. The fact that you are trying to learn their language means a lot to them.

When you first meet with your management group, the most important task is to gain their confidence and respect. The Mexicans will view you first as a person and only secondly as part of the company and will expect you to do the same with them.

Trying to launch immediately into your executive role needlessly risks alienating them—which is what I did and created all kinds of unnecessary problems. If you relax, show your genuine interest in them as people, and take your time getting to the management issues, you'll gain their trust. Once they see you're basically a nice guy, you have surmounted the first and most important hurdle.

I was certainly an example of what not to do when I arrived. As you may recall, I jumped straight into work issues on the first day. I can imagine now how the managers must have felt. I should, of course, have had an initial informal meeting just to get to know them a little and let them see me as a person. And how I needed even a little Spanish! It would have made it so much easier to understand how the Mexicans think and to benefit from their knowledge and experience. One mistake I believe I also made was to say what *I* thought first. After that they would not dare say anything which did not agree with my opinion, so I never really found out what they thought. I think it is a problem we all tend to have coming from the States. We aren't aware of how a person can be put off when we express our views first.

Here are some things to watch in the actual work situation. You have no idea what I went through trying to find out what the problem was when something went wrong. At first they'll just smile and tell you what they think you want to hear. Mexicans are renowned for their personal sensitivity. Tread lightly and be patient. I had to learn the hard way not to just come right out and say what I thought. Objectively pointing out what's wrong may be a good way to get improvements in the States, but it just hurts people's feelings in Mexico.

There will, of course, be times when you have to criticize somebody. Make sure you do it in private and with the utmost diplomacy. Never accuse anyone outright of being in the wrong, for instance, and when you do have to criticize, never do it in front of others. In Mexico that makes for a really serious loss of face and will raise almost insurmountable barriers to getting the improvements you want.

You may recall from my previous letter that I committed exactly this error. Not only did I criticize the supervisor in front of the workers, but later on I directly accused the production manager of making a mistake in his report. Now I understand why the supervisor was absent from work due to "illness" for two days. He had completely lost face with his workers and colleagues—and imagine how long that takes to rebuild! I certainly know better now. When I see something wrong on the plant floor, I quickly draw the manager away from the group and point out that "we have a problem" and leave it to him to solve—not single him out and blame him on the spot. He knows very well he is to blame, but cannot voice it. Problems certainly have been solved much more quickly and effectively since I have understood how to handle their sensitivities.

There are major operational difficulties which result from Mexican cultural traditions and management practices. But they will not simply go away with the application of the management techniques we've been trained in. You've got to adapt them to the Mexican scene. Look at all breakdowns from this perspective before you act. By listening carefully, I've come up with some good ideas for problem solving that may be a bit unorthodox, but the ideas frequently work because they fit the Mexican way of doing things. After all, they've lived with these difficulties for a long time, and many are aware of how they disrupt efficient business operations.

For example, the way they work in teams is very different from ours. We are used to a democratic approach, where the decision of the majority defines what we decide to do. That does not work here. If everyone is not in agreement, the job does not get done correctly because the ones who do not agree will often not make any effort. So the whole thing breaks down.

So watch what's going on, ask questions, and listen carefully. When it's time to make changes, involve the Mexican managers as fully as possible in identifying the problems and working out solutions.

After all, they're the ones who will have to convince the workers to make the changes that are needed. Trying to change things without the involvement and support of your managers just doesn't work in Mexico.

Also, keep strictly to the lines of authority. Bypassing someone in the chain of command is a good way to make an unnecessary enemy.

Overall, your best strategy is praise. Mexicans are really responsive to being appreciated. It is absolutely the best motivation, especially when done publicly.

Above all, in your everyday work, be flexible and open-minded. Remember, you have to accept that things are done differently here. If you insist on having everything your way, you will seem unreasonable and lose the support of your Mexican managers. Finally—and at the risk of repeating myself—I want to underline the importance of good human relations in the Mexican work situation. At home we are more willing to work with someone we don't like provided that person is competent; after all, we are paid to do a job. Mexicans, on the other hand, have to feel comfortable with the people they work with if they are to give their best; hence, the greater importance of human relations.

Well, Bob, I hope this will help get you started on the right foot. I certainly wish someone had been around to help point me in the right direction. It would have saved me many a sleepless night and would have made me a far more effective manager from the start. I look forward very much to seeing you soon.

Sincerely,

John

Another Letter from Sr. González

Dear Pablo,

How are you? Elena and I certainly miss you and María. How are the boys? Has Juan fully recovered from his injury? I know it was only minor, but you must allow his godfather to express his concern.

It certainly has been a long time since I last wrote to you. You ask how things have been going at the plant, and I must confess I have had many frustrating experiences. But at the same time, I am beginning to appreciate the need for some of the things our North American general manager is trying to do. They have undoubtedly improved our operation. Some of my change in attitude can be traced to a very fortuitous event that occurred some time ago.

Quite by accident one evening, the manager and I actually had a talk. It was at the end of the day and he looked especially tired, but at the same time he seemed to be more relaxed than usual. Anyway, he stopped at my office door to talk for a minute and then invited me for a drink. I was quite surprised because he'd never before shown much interest in socializing with me—or anyone else in the office. But that night we both opened up and talked almost like friends. It was quite remarkable, and I think we both learned a lot. We even laughed at some of the misunderstandings we'd had in the past! Since then, there have been many improvements, and I finally feel we are working together rather than at odds—most of the time anyway.

It was certainly interesting to hear that you are thinking of joining a U.S. firm. If it is not presumptuous of me, I wonder if it might be helpful if I give you a few pointers which, if I'd had them a year ago, would have saved a lot of anguish.

The first thing you have to know about working for an American is that the job (and getting it done) is foremost in his mind. As amazing as it may sound, the North American on the job is completely able to set aside personal relationships. He doesn't really care what you're like as long as you accomplish what you're expected to. And make a note of this—he's impressed by what you actually achieve, not by what you intend to do or say you can do. Putting into words your ideas (and ideals) and your ambitions, which we Mexicans consider necessary in launching any project, gets no credit from the North American. And be careful what you say about when the job will be done. He will hold you to it, down to the last detail. Make sure you are always on the safe side when estimating the time a task should take. Allow yourself a cushion in case of unforeseen setbacks. Also, if you run into any delays, be sure to tell him *immediately*. In most cases he will be quite considerate and gladly help you with the problem. But never come with an excuse after the fact— he will be furious!

As you know, we are used to saying yes to everything the boss tells us without thinking if we fully understand it, or if it is even possible to do—just as we did with Mr. Smith when he told us to go ahead on our own to implement the new procedures. He believed us when we said "yes, we can do it" (and I guess most of us hoped we could), but look what happened! The truth is that some of us didn't fully understand exactly what he wanted, and some of us were afraid to do anything until he gave orders to begin. The same thing kept happening with the monthly reports at first. We would always (with the best of intentions) say "yes, yes, they will be ready on time"—and they rarely were. We just didn't make the effort to estimate carefully how long it would realistically take to do, nor did we anticipate the inevitable problems which always come up. Now we are learning. We tell the boss when we aren't sure we can meet a deadline and then agree on one we know we can make, plus we are much more open with questions and getting clarification before committing ourselves. This certainly has changed the tense atmosphere. Work is also improving, the day-to-day operations are much smoother; and, as you can imagine, we all feel much better about our work and are beginning to really appreciate our boss.

Make sure you understand exactly what your responsibilities are. Ask questions until you're certain about what is expected of you, and bear in mind that you are held in higher esteem if you admit that you do not fully understand something than if you attempt to go ahead without sufficient explanation and something goes wrong. Then plan your work in detail, check to make sure the plan is followed, and follow up and check again all the jobs you have delegated. Remember, when the North American executive delegates a responsibility to you, that means you will be personally held accountable for everything that happens in your area, even if one of your workers does something wrong.

We have certainly learned to check and recheck our own work as well as that of our subordinates. As you may recall in my last letter, we had several cases where something went wrong, and we (the managers) were not on top of the situation. Of course, we realize now that the problem was that we weren't really training our people well enough, nor working closely enough with them to give them the encouragement and confidence in themselves they needed. Now we spend almost all our time on the plant floor "where the action is" making sure our people understand exactly what they are doing and giving them support in their efforts. It has made a big difference in their attitude toward their work and a big improvement in their productivity as well as in the quality of our products.

The American executive expects some errors to be made, and you will not lose his respect if you openly admit when you have made a mistake (as long as it does not happen too often). Remember the American manager is more concerned with solving a problem and getting on with the job than with fixing blame.

Keep in mind also that he wants and needs to know your views on all work questions, even if they don't agree with his own. He particularly needs, and will value, your knowledge of the Mexican work environment.

Expressing our real views, of course, is difficult and, as you may recall, at first we kept quiet and waited for the boss to tell us what he wanted. Sometimes we were very worried because we knew that the way Mr. Smith wanted to do a job doesn't work in Mexico, but we didn't dare to say anything. Fortunately, now we have the confidence to give our opinion without fear of him getting cross, and he really appreciates it. I think it is a shyness we have to overcome. In doing so we could help prevent many problems for American managers when they come to Mexico.

One of the hardest things I had to learn was that our manager wanted to be kept informed about everything that was going on, good or bad, and that he wouldn't be upset by negative comments or information. Indeed, it earned his respect. I think that's a trait Mexican businessmen would be wise to cultivate.

I guess the final thing to remember is that North Americans, even though they seem cold and hard to get to know, can be OK guys—just like Mexicans!—when you get below the surface.

Pablo, I hope these pointers will help you in your new job. I wish someone had given me some of this advice when I started. My very best wishes in your new adventure, and I hope you will be very happy. Please give my warmest greetings to María and the boys.

Affectionately,

Luís

Appendix A

Keys to a Successful Assignment in Mexico

Based on the preceding discussion, it is clear that the success of a business operation in Mexico depends overwhelmingly on the executive charged with the responsibility for its overall management. It is thus essential that the executive who is to serve in Mexico be given every possible support for a successful assignment. The home office of the corporation is responsible for ensuring that this support is available prior to departure and during the executive's stay abroad. The following are considered to be the key factors in creating an environment for success:

1. Selection
2. Preparation
3. Communication with the head office

1. Selection

Here are some of the most important traits for the American being assigned to Mexico. The person selected should be:

a. Flexible (with a spouse who is flexible)

b. Sincerely interested in Mexico and its culture

c. Ready to study Spanish intensively

d. Modest about his/her own country and culture

e. Receptive to the personal growth potential of the assignment

f. Skilled in the human relations side of management

The last point is especially important. Mexican executives and their U.S. counterparts with experience in Mexico agree that this is the *key to adaptation*, and that, where interpersonal relations skills are present, the American will be able to overcome most of the hurdles caused by differences in culture and management style. Here are a few of the many comments by the managers interviewed which underline this point:

> "Many Mexicans are reluctant to work for U.S. companies because of their lack of attention to human relations."(M)[1]

> "The biggest problem for most Americans is their lack of regard for human relations." (U)

> "Once human relations policies are put into place, all other problems tend gradually to fade away." (U)

> "The American materialistic outlook has given rise to tremendous efficiency and productivity, much of it, however, at the expense of human relations." (M)

> "The U.S. executive must recognize and accept a totally different culture below the Rio Grande and must be willing to adapt to it."(U)

2. Preparation

A substantive cross-cultural briefing (for executive and spouse—and children as well) with Mexican informants is especially important. Discussions based on the material presented in this book would be particularly appropriate. The executive should read all the reports available and have ample opportunity to talk with the person leaving the position (taking care to withhold judgments based on that person's negative comments).

---

[1]Comment by (U), U.S. executive; by (M), Mexican executive.

Other things to do:

a. Read a good book on Mexican history and culture. Also, keep up with current economic, social, and political developments in Mexico.

b. Begin studying Spanish intensively. It is desirable to have a working knowledge of the language on arrival if at all possible.

c. Take an orientation trip to Mexico and talk with Mexicans and Americans about the Mexican business scene.

3. Communication with the Head Office

Part of the frustration experienced by U.S. managers working for U.S. corporations in Mexico is caused by what they see as the lack of understanding at the head office for the special circumstances at the Mexican plant. In other words, head office decisions made in a culturally isolated environment sometimes contribute more to the failure of an operation than to its success. In order to make sound decisions based on a knowledge and understanding of the Mexican environment, head office staff also need cross-cultural orientation.[2] Above all, the head office must have full confidence in the judgment of its local manager and let that person have a great deal of leeway in the management of the operation. These conditions were met in all the outstandingly successful operations studied.

A note on the preparation of Mexican executives: Mexicans joining a U.S. firm in Mexico should do a number of the same things recommended for their U.S. counterparts, e.g., participate in a substantive briefing on cross-cultural relations with Americans; read up on U.S. history, culture, and current affairs; polish their English; talk with Mexican and U.S. managers about U.S. business activity in Mexico; and visit the United States.

---

[2]This fact emerged clearly and explicitly from the interviews.

Appendix B

Research Methodology

The most complex part of the research that led to this book proved to be the series of in-depth interviews with Mexican and U.S. executives. It is these interviews that are dealt with in this appendix.

Special Considerations

1. All interviews had to be arranged through personal introductions. This is a necessity in the Mexican cultural environment. Otherwise, interviews would either not be granted or they would take place in an atmosphere of suspicion, which would make it impossible to elicit reliable information.

2. Because of the sensitive nature of all aspects of cultural interaction between the U.S. and Mexico, special precautions had to be taken in structuring and conducting the interviews. It was often necessary to depart from the prepared questionnaire, and frequently the interviewer had to gauge whether what was said was as important as how it was said.

3. On most of the topics investigated, there existed little or no published data on the Mexican side. This made it necessary to interview a much larger number of Mexican executives (80% of the total) than American. Many of the executives interviewed had the experience of working in more than one region of Mexico, and in those cases they were encouraged to talk about regional differences.

Focus of the Study

1. The objective of the study was to produce a handbook on cross-cultural management for U.S. and Mexican business executives. To achieve this, the research instrument had to be sharply focused on practical management concepts. It also had to be succinct so as to be quickly read and reread by busy executives. The reader is assumed to have considerable background in management theory and practice. Readers without this background are referred to the relevant texts in the bibliography.

2. Similarly, since the intention was to produce a succinct handbook, the author has purposely avoided delving more than absolutely necessary into the underlying sociological and psychological dimensions of cross-cultural relationships. It is hoped that this book will stimulate further research and publication on these subjects.

3. Mexico is in a state of rapid development which is constantly changing the attitudes and practices of the business community. It is to be expected that the analysis undertaken in this study will have to be expanded and elaborated on over the course of time.

Selection of Regions for the Study

Mexico is a country of enormous variety in its people and in their outlook and attitudes toward work. As it would have been impossible to cover all the regions of the country in one brief volume, a choice had to be made. Since by far the greatest interaction between U.S. and Mexican executives takes place in the manufacturing industries, regions showing the highest concentration of such industries were identified as possible foci for the study. For the sake of economy, three regions were chosen:

1. Monterrey and Nuevo León, representing the north

2. Guadalajara and Jalisco, representing the center

3. Mexico City and its metropolitan area

For the reasons set forth in the introduction to the book, the region comprising the oil-rich states along the Gulf of Mexico was not included. There are other industrially important areas, such as the states of Puebla and Morelos in the south, Querétaro and Guanajuato in the center, and Baja California in the north, which possess special characteristics. Although these could not be treated in detail here, most of the cultural and management-style characteristics dealt with in this book also apply to a greater or lesser extent to those areas.

Selection of Companies and Executives

The selection of the companies to be included was based on the following criteria:

1. Nature of the business (over 80% of the companies were from the manufacturing sector)
2. Size of the company
3. Blend of companies in the region (e.g., a greater number of medium-sized firms in Guadalajara, mostly large firms in Monterrey)

Executives to be interviewed were selected using the following criteria:

1. Company size and type
2. Position held
3. Length of executive service
4. Nationality

Length of executive service was considered an important criterion insofar as it affected the breadth and variety of the executive's experience.

Analysis of the Interviews

Of the 72 interviews, 37 took place in Guadalajara. However, 5 of the executives concerned had also worked in Monterrey and Mexico City. In Monterrey only 10 executives were interviewed, but these covered a representative cross-section of companies—all large. In Mexico City 25 executives were interviewed, again representing a cross-section of interests, with emphasis on larger companies. Of the total, 52 were Mexican, 17 were from the United States and 3 were from other countries (see table I).

For the Mexican interviewees, the average executive business experience was 18.6 years. For the expatriate executives it was 20.5 years. As mentioned above, length of executive experience was considered an important factor in ensuring considerable exposure to practical management problems (see table II).

Human resources directors represent the largest number of executives interviewed (53%). This was considered desirable in view of the nature of the study. Next came general managers (30.5%) and, lastly, owners of businesses (11.2%) (see table III).

Company size. The companies were separated into three categories, according to the number of employees. Companies with over 500 employees were classified as large, those with 200 to 500 employees as medium-sized, and those with under 200 as small. Based on these categories, 55% of the companies involved were large, 33% were medium-sized, and 12% were small (see table IV). It should be noted that this distribution is in no way meant to represent the distribution of companies by size on a national scale but was the result of selecting companies with cross-cultural interests and whose executives had extensive and varied experience.

Methodology

Questionnaire and outline. Having obtained a personal introduction from a person well-known to the executive to be interviewed, it was still necessary to give the interviewee some preparation in order to gain his confidence. Thus, each executive was provided with (1) an outline of the purpose and scope of the study, giving the anticipated contents of the proposed book and (2) a copy of the questionnaire to be used in the interview. As a result, the executives were ready to contribute considerable time to the interview, in most cases over two hours. The questionnaire was drawn up with the assistance of Dr. Roger Chartier (see below for an outline of the questionnaire).

Analysis of the data. Based on the questionnaire, the data were separated into appropriate sections. Other subjects, not specifically mentioned in the questionnaire but consistently brought out in the interviews, were added. Most data could be analyzed objectively, but some were subjective in nature. Fortunately, on these issues there was almost complete agreement among the interviewees. This did, however, place a great responsibility on the author to avoid any value judgments or opinions of her own. In order to ensure as far as possible the validity and objectivity of the interpretation and presentation, the draft manuscript was submitted to a number of critics from the business and academic communities. Both Mexican and U.S. critics overwhelmingly endorsed the findings and, as a result, they may be confidently presented to the public.

Table I

Executives Interviewed

Nationality	Region[a]			Total
	A	B	C	
Mexican	25	17	10	52
U.S.	10	7	0	17
Other	2	1	0	3
Total	37	25	10	72

Table II

Years of Business Experience

Nationality	Region[a]			Total
	A	B	C	
Mexican	14-25	12-20	13-20	18.6
U.S.	16-25	18-30	—	20.5
Other	25-30	20	—	23.5
Total Avg.	21.3	19.0	17.0	20.9

Table III

Positions Held

Nationality	Executive Position			Total
	Owner	Genl. Mgr.	Dir. H.R.	
Mexican	5	11	36	52
U.S.	1	10	6	17
Other	2	1	—	3
Total	8	22	42	72

Table IV

Company Size

	Region[a]			
Size	A	B	C	Total
Large (over 500)	13	18	9	40
Medium (200-500)	17	6	1	24
Small (under 200)	7	1	—	8
Total	37	25	10	72

Source: Kras, E. S., "The Effects of Culture on Management Style: A Comparative Study—Mexico-U.S.A.," paper read at 1987 Business Association of Latin American Studies (BALAS) Conference, American Graduate School of International Management (AGSIM), Phoenix, Arizona.

[a]Regions: A=Guadalajara, B=Mexico City, C=Monterrey.

Critics. The eight critics who generously gave of their time to review the text in draft form represented the three regions studied. Of the total, six were business executives and two were university professors. Four of the reviewers were Mexican, three were from the United States, and one was from Canada. Their suggestions and encouragement were invaluable in helping me refine the first draft of the book. The reviewers were as follows: Clifford Cameron, S.H.M. (Chemical) Company, Mexico City; Roger Chartier, Universidad Autónoma de Guadalajara; Roberto Santa Cruz, Grupo SERCAM, Guadalajara; Enrique Luis González Garza, Acumuladores Monterrey, Monterrey; Adolf Horn, American Chamber of Commerce, Guadalajara; Enrique Lazcano, Universidad Autónoma de Guadalajara; José Luís Reyes, UNISYS Corporation, Guadalajara; and Hubert Smiley, Universidad Autónoma de Guadalajara.

Comments. This study has been extremely instructive insofar as it enabled the author to develop an interviewing technique adapted to Mexican conditions. At the outset no information was available on the problems of obtaining meaningful data in the area of the behavioral sciences in a Latin American setting. The interviewing technique had to be perfected by trial and error, and it was found that it had to be kept highly flexible so as to remain responsive to the cultural environment.

Here the author's interviewing experience as a human resources executive proved invaluable.

In addition the study has produced a framework which enables management styles and cultural factors present in two different cultures to be directly compared. It is hoped this effort will provide both a structure for and a stimulus to further research in this field.

Outline of the Questionnaire

Give a brief history of the company.

Organization

1. Briefly describe the organizational structure.
2. What is your general area of responsibility?
3. What is your general area of authority?
4. Is any authority delegated to lower levels?
5. How do employees feel about responsibility they were given (attitude toward accountability)?

Staffing

1. Selection and recruitment:
   a. How do you find new staff?
   b. On what basis is selection made (family, friends)?
   c. What method of selection do you consider most reliable?
2. What do you consider the most important reason for turnover?
3. What do you consider the most important reason for absenteeism?
4. What are the possibilities of mobility in the company?
5. Which is more important to a new employee—job content? interest? salary? some other factor?

Direction, Supervision, Motivation

1. What is your view on:
   a. dedication of employees to their job?
   b. dependability of employees?
   c. initiative of employees?
2. What factors (external or internal) do you think most affect the employee's attitude toward his or her work?
3. What is employee attitude toward punctuality? What is your opinion?
4. Is counseling and evaluation of staff done formally or as you feel necessary?
5. How do staff members feel about evaluations?
6. Does religion play an important part in the work situation?
7. Do employees feel more loyalty toward their superior or toward the company?
8. What is the attitude of employees toward competition within? outside?
9. What is your view on the level of cooperation between:
   a. manager and employee?
   b. employee and employee (same and different departments)?
   c. employee and manager of different departments?
10. For what reasons do you terminate an employee?

Labor Unions

1. What effect do labor unions have on management? on staff?

General

1. What do you feel is the most difficult problem to deal with when working in Mexico?
2. What do you feel is the most difficult adjustment that the Mexican executive has to make when dealing with executives from the United States?

Selected Bibliography

Ardilla Espinel, Noé. "Criterios y Valores de la Cultura Anglo-Sajo-Americana y la Cultura Latina." *Revista Latino-Americana de Psicología* 14 (1982).

Arias Galicia, Fernando, coord. *Administración de Recursos Humanos.* México City: Ed. Trillas, 1980.

Blanchard, Kenneth, and Johnson Spencer. *The One-Minute Manager.* New York: Morrow, 1982.

————. *Putting the One-Minute Manager to Work.* New York: Blanchford Management Corp., 1984.

Bloom, Allan. *Closing of the American Mind.* New York: Simon and Schuster, 1990.

Carlisle, Arthur E. "Cultural Differences and Supervisory Styles." *Industrial Relations Quarterly Review* 23 (1968).

Chamberlain, Neil W. *Remaking American Values.* New York: Basic Books, 1977.

Chartier, Roger. "Bilingualism in Quebec Business." *Industrial Relations Quarterly Review* 23 (1968).

Clark, Jane. "Culture: The Essential Dimension of Development." *Beshara Magazine.* Reprinted in *Noetic Sciences Review,* no. 20 (1991).

Condon, John C. *Good Neighbors: Communicating with the Mexicans.* Yarmouth, ME: Intercultural Press, 1985.

Craig, Robert L., and Lester R. Bittel. *Training and Development Handbook.* New York: McGraw-Hill, 1971.

Crocker, Olga, Cyril Dharney, and Johnny Sik Leung Chiu. *Quality Circles.* New York: Methuen, 1984.

Cumberland, Charles. *Mexico, the Struggle for Modernity.* New York: Oxford University Press, 1968.

Davis, Stanley M. *Comparative Management: Organizational and Cultural Perspectives.* Englewood Cliffs, NJ: Prentice-Hall, 1971.

Diaz Ramirez, Alberto. *Como Conducir Juntas.* México City: Ed. Limusa, 1983.

Dowling, Peter J., and Randall S. Schuler. *Human Resource Management.* Boston: PWS-Kent, 1990.

Drucker, Peter. *The Changing World of the Executive.* New York: Times Books, 1982.

Ferner, Jack D. *Successful Time Management.* New York: John Wiley, 1980.

Fite, Gilbert C., and Jim E. Courtland. *An Economic History of the United States.* Boston: Houghton Mifflin, 1973.

Fuentes Mares, José. *La Revolución Mexicana.* México: Ed. Joaquín Mortiz, 1971.

Furer, Arthur. *La Empresa Multinacional y los Estados Nacionales.* Ph.D. diss., Universidad Autónoma de Guadalajara, 1975.

González Pineda, Francisco. *El Mexicano: La Psicología de su Destructividad.* México City: Ed. Pax, 1975.

Harman, Willis, and John Hormann. *Creative Work: The Constructive Role of Business in Transforming Society.* Indianapolis, IN: Knowledge Systems, Inc., 1990.

Harris, Philip R., and Robert T. Moran. *Managing Cultural Differences,* (2d rev. ed.). Houston: Gulf Publishing, 1986.

Hecht, Maurice R. *What Happens in Management.* New York: American Management Association, 1984.

Hernandez Medina, Alberto, and Luis Narro Rodriguez. *Comosomos Los Mexicanos.* México City: Centro de Estudios Educativos, A.C., and Consejo Nacional de Recursos para la Atencion de la Juventud, 1987.

Hoopes, David S. "Intercultural Communication Concepts and the Psychology of Intercultural Experience." In Margaret D. Pusch, (Ed.). *Multicultural Education: A Cross-Cultural Training Approach.* Yarmouth, ME: Intercultural Press, 1979.

Iturriaga, J. *La Estructura y Cultura de México.* México: Fondo de Cultura Económica, 1951.

Kliksberg, Bernardo. *Administración, Subdesarrollo y Estrangulamiento Económico.* Buenos Aires: Ed. Paidos, 1972.

Kras, Eva S. *Modernizing of Mexican Management Styles.* Las Cruces, NM: Editts, 1994.

—————. *Cultura Gerencial—México-E.U.A.* Guadalajara: Harper & Row Latinoamericana, 1987.

—————. "Cultural Awareness Pays in Mexican Workplace." *Business Mexico* 3 (1986).

—————. "The Effects of Culture on Management Style: A Comparative Study—Mexico-U.S.A." In *Proceedings.* Lubbock, TX: Business Association of Latin American Studies (BALAS), 1987.

—————. "Los Gerentes Mexicanos: Están en Condiciones de Competir?" *Ejecutivos de Finanzas* 16 (1987).

—————. "Maquiladora Management—Problems of Working in Two Cultures." *Maquiladora Newsletter* 14, nos. 5, 6, 7 (1987).

Lafaye, Jacques. *Quetzalcoatl et Guadalupe.* Paris: Ed. Gallimard, 1974.

Marett, Robert. *Mexico.* London: Thames & Hudson, 1971.

Massie, Joseph L., and Jan Lutyes. *Management in an International Context.* New York: Harper & Row, 1972.

Orr, Paul Glenn. *Dependent Schooling Abroad and the United States Corporation.* Washington, DC: U.S. Department of State and University of Alabama, 1980.

Ortiz, Edgar, and Donald Hudson. *Perspectivas Ideológicas e Instituciónales Hacia 1990: Análisis de actitudes y opiniónes y sus implicaciónes en la administración.* México City: UNAM, 1980.

Ouchi, William G. *Theory Z.* New York: Avon Books, 1981.

Paz, Octavio. *El Laberinto de la Soledad*. México City: Fondo de Cultura Económica, 1959.

————. *Posdata*. México: Veintiuno Editoriales, 1970.

Peters, Thomas, and Robert Waterman. *In Search of Excellence*. New York: Warner Books, 1984.

Ray, Michael, and Alan Ringler, (eds.). *The New Paradigm in Business*. New York: Putnam, 1993.

Rehder, Robert R. *Latin-American Management Development and Performance*. Reading, MA: Addison-Wesley, 1968.

Reyes Ponce, Agustin. *El Análisis de Puestos*. México City: Ed. Limusa, 1983.

Riding, Alan. *Distant Neighbors, a Portrait of the Mexicans*. New York: Alfred E. Knopf, 1984.

Rossi, Flavia de. *El Empresario Mexicano*. México City: UNAM, 1977.

Sechrest, William B. *Six Global Business Trends: A Lesson in Interconnectedness*. San Francisco: World Business Academy Perspectives 6, no. 3.

Siliceo, Alfonso A. *Capacitación y Desarrollo de Personal*. México City: Ed. Limusa, 1983.

Soria Murillo, Victor M. *Relaciónes Humanas, Teoria y Casos*. México City: Ed. Limusa, 1983.

Stewart, Edward C., and Milton J. Bennett. *American Cultural Patterns: A Cross-Cultural Perspective*, (rev. ed.). Yarmouth, ME: Intercultural Press, 1991.

Vázquez, Josefina, and Lorenzo Meyer. *México Frente Estados Unidos*. México City: Colegio de México, 1983.

Walton, Mary. *The Deming Management Method*. New York: Dodd, Mead, 1986.